SELECTION FOR
INDUSTRIAL LEADERSHIP

SELECTION FOR
INDUSTRIAL LEADERSHIP

by

A. G. ARBOUS

GREENWOOD PRESS, PUBLISHERS
WESTPORT, CONNECTICUT

This work was undertaken in the National Institute for Personnel Research, and is published in association with the South African Council for Scientific and Industrial Research.

Originally published in 1953
by Oxford University Press, Capetown, London, New York

Reprinted with the permission
of Oxford University Press

First Greenwood Reprinting 1971

Library of Congress Catalogue Card Number 77-110266

SBN 8371-4492-2

Printed in the United States of America

PREFACE

THE TECHNIQUE OF Situational Testing for Leadership owes its origin to World War II, when the British War Office and the American Office of Strategic Services developed what have now become known as socio-dramatic and sociometric test procedures. Their object was to assess the suitability and potentialities of men as officers, and for special assignments in secret service and intelligence work.

The need for adequate personality and character assessment in this field was obvious. Existing techniques for this purpose left much to be desired. An attempt was therefore made to devise some method which was less artificial, indirect and susceptible to spurious errors in its application than the customary questionnaires and self-rating techniques. Moreover, leadership was regarded, not merely as a general psychological quality consisting of a complex pattern of personality attributes, but also as a 'social value', situationally determined.

By placing a candidate in a socio-dramatic situation which simulated that in which he would be expected to operate in the field; and by systematizing the observations of skilled assessors on his performance and mode of reaction, it was thought that a more realistic estimate of his leadership potentialities in that field would be obtained. Furthermore, by skilful scene-shifting, an infinite variety of socio-dramatic situations could be devised, each of which would contribute additional information on some facet of personality make-up.

Testing of this nature was justified on *a priori* psychological grounds, and was included in a test battery containing more conventional material, e.g. pencil-and-paper tests of general and specific abilities, projective techniques and clinical interview assessments. The whole programme was an elaborate affair, conducted on residential lines at a testing centre or guest-house. The expense involved was considered to be justified by the anticipated gains in the correct placement of individuals in high-level assignments, where failure would result in serious consequences.

The rationale of these procedures and the experience gained during their application was so convincing that, after the War, they were adapted to the needs of industry. The method used by the British Civil Service has been the most notable.

Until quite recently, however, the scientific justification for their use has rested on grounds of face-validity only. Many thorny problems and insuperable difficulties have beset the path of strict validation, and controversy on the subject has been keen in some quarters.

When a unique opportunity is suddenly presented for research, it so often happens that the research worker, much to his chagrin, is not in a position to take it. An exception to this occurred at the end of 1948, when the N.I.P.R. was requested to assist in the selection of administrative trainees for a large industrial corporation in South Africa. When the number of applicants increased to 500, and when management took the decision that, for reasons of internal policy, all of the 146 applicants who were existing employees should be fully tested, I realized that a golden opportunity was at hand. I was immediately struck by the possibility of overcoming one of the major obstacles which had prevented scientific validation of these procedures in the past, viz. that a follow-up study could only be carried out on the selected group which was naturally small and highly restricted in range of ability. Correction for this factor in one's predictions is only permissible provided certain conditions hold—and these are so often violated that the research worker is left helpless. In this case, if the selected trainees together with the remaining employee-candidates were a representative sample of the total group tested, the need for correction for restriction in range would fall away, and a validation study along traditional lines could be undertaken.

My publication of this work is, therefore, prompted by these favourable circumstances.

On the other hand, there are certain limitations to this research project which should not be overlooked. The N.I.P.R. was in fact faced with two tasks which had to be performed simultaneously:

(a) that of an applied nature which involved the use of unvalidated test procedures for the selection of suitable candidates;

(b) that of a research nature whereby the validity of the selection procedures themselves would be tested.

The interests of the N.I.P.R. were quite naturally concentrated on the latter, while those of the sponsor firm were centred primarily in the former. While these interests are not mutually exclusive they are not always mutually compatible, and in many respects research interests have to give way to the demands of practical requirements. This situation is paradoxical in nature, for on the one hand, research is only possible because an applied job has to be done, whereas on the other hand, research cannot proceed in certain directions because of the same reason, which prevents an adherence to strict scientific procedure. In many respects the investigation was caught in this conflict, and the point is emphasized at the outset so that the reader may appreciate why this project did not take the course of an ideally planned experiment. While the Corporation went out of its way to oblige in the provision of research facilities, there are obvious limitations beyond which it would be unreasonable to expect any sponsor to go. The N.I.P.R. was thus compelled to cut the 'research' coat according to the 'applied' cloth, and in doing so was grateful for the provision of a generous bolt of material. This was far in excess of that needed merely to fulfil the Corporation's own needs of selection.

In carrying out this research I have used criteria of a circumscribed nature. This has both advantages and deficiencies. By defining quite specifically just what is being predicted one gains in precision, but at the same time loses generality in one's statements. I consider, however, that there is no point in trying to stretch one's findings beyond the limits of the data. The scientist will have to be patient before greater claims can be made for these procedures.

In dealing with the subject-matter of this work, I have laid emphasis on the psychometric, as opposed to the subjective, approach to the assessment of test performance. This will, no doubt, give rise to controversy, and many may well question the application of this method in practical assessment programmes. I do not wish to suggest that the assessment of men should be undertaken purely in this impersonal and mechanical fashion in terms of a single index—the test battery score—although in our present state of ignorance this may well be the only approach which can be scientifically justified. Neither in the present instance, nor on subsequent applications of the battery was a strict psychometric approach adopted. The final report on a candidate submitted to the sponsor, in addition to test-profile, final score, and probability of 'success', consisted of a subjective evaluation of (I) Educational Background, (II) Occupational Record, (III) Sociological Background, and (IV) Clinical Assessment of Personality Make-Up.

It is regretted that the possible recognition of candidates has precluded the publication of samples of individual reports, together with the Corporation's own evaluation after completion of the training period.

My reason for dealing chiefly with the psychometric approach is that I wished to confine myself to conclusions which could be satisfactorily demonstrated, and to avoid the unnecessary obtrusion of untested hypotheses in a field where these have been all too prevalent. Sufficient data were simply not available to test strictly the validity of clinical observations on items of personality make-up. To have dealt loosely, in terms of subjective impression, with the accuracy of the diagnosis of personality defects, and a prognosis of their consequences in the administrative field, would have marred the rigorous procedure which we have accepted as a standard for this work.

Finally, it has been my object to demonstrate both the advantages and limitations of test battery selection, for it is felt that the latter are not sufficiently recognized. The psychometric method is suited to this purpose. It is hoped that the illustrations contained in this work will encourage a more balanced attitude to test selection and classification. The techniques developed here will show how management policy can be designed in advance to meet specific needs. On the other hand they will discourage exaggerated claims by revealing just how inefficient predictions can be under certain circumstances.

The importance of material which usually eludes the psychometric approach, and which is carefully evaluated in the subjective, has not been overlooked in this work, where the relative merits and weaknesses of both systems have been enumerated.

It is my view that the gap between the two methodologies could be considerably narrowed, if exponents of the latter were less content to shelter behind the belief that clinical hypotheses cannot be so readily tested along psychometric lines. No real attempt has yet been made to include in the psychometric structure data which are normally made available under the headings listed above, and which form the basis for subjective assessment. A true appreciation of the accuracy and inefficiency of clinical prediction might well result from research in this field.

My own contribution to leadership testing is preceded by, I hope, an unbiased review of earlier work as far as this has been recorded in a series of scattered publications.

Whereas previous results have often been somewhat inadequately reported, I have attempted in this work to present my own research findings, and the development of new techniques, in a manner which can be closely checked and followed. By so doing I have sought to achieve a secondary objective: that of providing a blue-print for those who wish to develop the psychometric structure of their own batteries in whatever field they may be interested. This may be particularly useful in the case of the new screening technique which is capable of wide application.

Finally, I have in the Annexures included copies of the socio-dramatic tests specially constructed for this programme. The Sheltered Employment Story, in particular, has subsequently been adapted to serve the demands of several different selection programmes, and, with further ingenuity, may well serve the needs of others in the future.

A. G. ARBOUS

National Institute for Personnel Research,
S.A. Council for Scientific and Industrial Research
    12 *July* 1951

ACKNOWLEDGEMENTS

IN PRESENTING these research findings I should like, first and foremost, to acknowledge my indebtedness to the erstwhile staff of the British War Office, and Civil Service Selection Boards, as well as to the Office of Strategic Services in America. In many ways this publication should be dedicated to those whose pioneer work in this field, during and shortly after World War II, was the main source of inspiration for the testing techniques developed in the present research project.

Acknowledgements are due also to all who participated in this work and helped to bring it to a successful conclusion. In this regard I wish to express my appreciation of the generous facilities provided by the industrial corporation concerned (whose identity cannot be revealed here), and for the assistance given by those members of its staff with whom our research team was most closely associated. If any individuals are to be singled out in this respect, I should like to mention in particular: the Staff Assistant to the General Manager whose far-sighted planning of the Administrative Trainee Scheme created the opportunities for basic research into the selection procedures themselves; the Training Officer of the Personnel Department whose effective administration guaranteed the smooth flow of candidates through the testing programme, and also the other Assessors whose vigilance during the Social-Interaction Tests greatly enhanced the value of this essential part of the selection procedures.

Furthermore, I thank all officials who acted as Assessors during the follow-up studies by means of which the validity of the tests was estimated. Though this method of selection has been in use for some time overseas, its predictive value has not yet been fully established, and I am grateful for the active participation of officials which has made the present advance possible.

In that no applicant was under any compulsion as far as the N.I.P.R. was concerned to submit to testing, I should like to thank them, our 'sample population', for their ready co-operation in this work.

The research involved in this project was undertaken by the Industrial Research Team of the National Institute for Personnel Research. I am, therefore, indebted to the following Technical Assistants who applied the Pencil-and-Paper Tests, acted as assessors in several test situations, and took part in the Trial Interview specially designed for this programme: Mrs. J. Maree, Mrs. D. Pitt, Mrs. I. Bergh, Miss B. McKiever.

I particularly wish to thank Mrs. J. Maree for her accurate and painstaking assistance with the many laborious statistical computations.

I should like to acknowledge also the assistance given to this research team by other senior members of the N.I.P.R. staff, Mrs. M. Baehr and Mr. R. V. Sutton, who willingly withdrew from their own research commitments to help with the clinical interviews and the assessment of candidates in the group-test situations. Mr. J. O'Meara of the staff of the

Johannesburg Teachers Training College also rendered valuable help in this phase of the project.

I am, furthermore, indebted to the Research Officer in charge of the N.I.P.R. Statistical Research Team, Mr. H. S. Sichel, for statistical consultation, and his permission to report my use of those techniques accredited to him in the text, before some of these had been published in their own right. Much helpful advice concerning the use of other statistical techniques was also received from Mr. J. S. Maritz of the statistical staff.

The reproduction of diagrams was done by Mr. J. L. Turner and Mrs. A. J. Neilson, whose neat and accurate work is greatly appreciated.

I am grateful also to Mr. J. E. Kerrich of the Sub-Department of Statistics of the University of the Witwatersrand, whose incisive comments of the work in manuscript form have contributed to a strict and unbiased presentation of the research findings.

In that every research worker depends on the critical faculties of another to enable him to articulate his ideas in the planning of a research project, and the development of new techniques, I wish to thank my Director, Dr. S. Biesheuvel, for allowing my free encroachment on his time for this purpose, as well as for his active participation in the clinical interviews and group tests, and his review of this manuscript before publication.

I wish to thank the following, and the authors concerned, for permission to quote from the publications listed in the references: American Psychological Association, Inc.; Industrial Welfare Society; National Institute of Industrial Psychology; Royal Medico-Psychological Association; The British War Office; The University of Chicago Press; University of London Press; *Journal of Consulting Psychology*, and the *Journal of Mental Science*.

Special acknowledgement is due to the authors and publishers of the following works which have been frequently quoted in the text:

    I. *Personnel Selection in the British Forces*, by P. E. Vernon and J. B. Parry; University of London Press Ltd., 1949.

    II. *Assessment of Men: Selection of Personnel for the Office of Strategic Services*, by the O.S.S. Assessment Staff; copyright, 1948, by Rinehart & Company, Inc., New York.

    III. *Personnel Selection: Test and Measurement Techniques*, by R. L. Thorndike; published by John Wiley & Sons, Inc., 1949.

    IV. 'The Validation of Civil Service Selection Board Procedures', by P. E. Vernon. *Occupational Psychology* XXIV, 75–95, 1950. (By permission of the C.I.S.S.B. Psychological Office.)

A. G. ARBOUS

National Institute for Personnel Research,
S.A. Council for Scientific and Industrial Research
    12 *July* 1951

CONTENTS

ANNEXURES PAGE

LIST OF DIAGRAMS

B: Diagrams in Appendix

CHAPTER I

INTRODUCTION

1. THE NATURE OF THE PROJECT

IN TERMS of the contract between a large South African industrial corporation and the Council for Scientific and Industrial Research, the National Institute for Personnel Research was requested during July 1948 to assist in the selection of candidates for an Administrative Trainee Scheme, to be inaugurated by the Corporation early in 1949. The main purpose of this scheme was to select up to thirty suitably qualified young men for an intensive period of training in various branches of administrative work, with a view to building up a reserve of capable and adequately trained employees, from among whom vacancies in 'top management' could be filled in the future. In order to place the selection of these trainees on as scientific a basis as possible, the N.I.P.R. was requested to put applicants through suitable selection procedures, and to make its recommendations to the Management Board.

The following principles, set out in the Corporation's Memorandum on the Administrative Trainee Scheme, provided a preliminary guide to the requirements demanded of trainees.*

It was recommended that candidates be selected from

(1) suitably qualified young men (graduates, or with qualifications such as C.A., A.S.A.A., C.W.A., C.I.S., and such other qualifications as may be approved from time to time) with or without experience, and

(2) existing employees who have shown exceptional promise, normally within the age and salary group of 30 years and £540 per annum.

Existing employees should receive special consideration, and special cases outside these limits should be considered on their merits. The ideal age and salary group is considered to be 22–25 years and £300–£360 per annum.

In this report emphasis was laid on the necessity for setting a high standard in the selection of candidates and of choosing men who would be capable, after adequate training, of measuring up to the demands of high-level administrative posts within the organization.

Before considering the problems facing the N.I.P.R. in the present instance, and the manner in which it set about tackling them, it is appropriate that we should review previous work done in this field in order to place this research project in its correct perspective.

* Annexure B to Management Board (Staff) Memorandum.

2. A REVIEW OF PREVIOUS WORK

Before World War II psychological testing had concentrated largely on the measurement of skills of the intellectual, perceptual and psycho-motor type. Psychological advances in the measurement of the conative and affective, as opposed to the cognitive side of man, had not been as great —not because of lack of interest, but chiefly because of the manifold difficulties presented by the problem of measuring the more intangible aspects of man's temperament, personality and character make-up. Quantification of data in this field had largely been confined to question-naires, rating scales and personality inventories. The inadequacy and unreliability of pre-war techniques of this type were soon appreciated by psychologists attempting to predict occupational success in fields where these qualities are important.

Thus in World War II psychologists were fairly well equipped to deal with the problems of selecting and classifying personnel for the lower occupational grades, where individual competence depended largely on, and could to a great extent be assessed in terms of, intellectual, perceptual and psycho-motor skills. The same could not, however, be said of their ability to select men to fill leadership roles in a warring society. As the need for individuals with these attributes was acutely felt, particularly after Dunkirk, the War Office was forced into the position of having to make adequate provision of officer personnel to lead its troops. Officer Cadet Training Units (O.C.T.U.s) had earlier been created to satisfy this need for competent personnel in the leadership categories.

As Vernon and Parry (1949)* point out (p. 52):

> The system worked fairly effectively so long as there was a large supply of good material, e.g. from the public schools. But when this source began to dry up, the boards, being faced with recruits whose social and educational backgrounds were entirely unfamiliar, were unable to discriminate effectively. Unsuitable candidates were often passed and sent to O.C.T.U. . . . where large proportions failed, with unfortunate effects on the morale of the remainder. Moreover, so many candidates who might have succeeded were rejected by the boards, often—according to their own accounts—on flimsy grounds such as grammar school education or socialist opinions, that recruits lost confidence in the system, and there was a real danger of insuf-ficient officers being forthcoming. Again, there was less opportunity than in 1914–18 for selection on the basis of performance in battle.

Gillman (1947) states that the wastage rate in training at the O.C.T.U.s where candidates had been selected by the old-type War Office Selection Boards varied between 20% and 40%.

At about this time an innovation was introduced in the British Army which was to have far-reaching consequences. Gillman (1947) reports that in June 1940 the first Area Psychiatrists in the United Kingdom were appointed. Despite expectations to the contrary and lack of encourage-ment, the psychiatric clinics which were set up were soon overwhelmed

---

* Quotations from this source are taken from *Personnel Selection in the British Forces* by permission of Messrs. P. E. Vernon and J. B. Parry and the University of London Press, Ltd.

with the number of cases to be dealt with. Service Psychiatrists dealing with these cases came to the conclusion that many could have been eliminated at the recruiting stage, for, with the aid of a personal history and an intelligence test, one could have foretold fairly accurately the future which they would have in the army. 'At the end of 1940, at the suggestion of a Command Psychiatrist, a Directorate of Officer Selection Personnel was set up, so that men joining the army would have their intelligence tested, and be interviewed by a personnel selection officer, and the dull and backward and the difficult cases interviewed by the psychiatrist, either for rejection from the army or for transfer to the unarmed or armed Pioneer Corps, or to any arm which was considered suitable.' (Gillman, 1947, p. 101.) This new approach to the problems of selection and classification was considered at the time to be a vast improvement on the earlier haphazard method. Success in this field encouraged the authorities to attempt an approach to the more difficult problem of officer selection, where personality factors and the attributes of leadership were the more important qualities to be assessed, and which in the past had eluded quantitative measurement.

Early in 1941 experiments were carried out by two psychiatrists attached to Scottish Command, encouraged by the G.O.C., Sir Andrew Thorne, who had previously been military attaché at Berlin and had observed some of the elaborate selection techniques developed by the German military psychologists. (Ansbacher, 1941; Burt, 1942; Farrago, 1941.) Officers attending courses at the Edinburgh Company Commanders School were given psychiatric interviews and intelligence tests, together with other tests on the German model. While the latter gave unpromising results, the correspondence between the psychiatric diagnoses and the school's estimates of the officers' worth was very striking. By 1942 the first experimental 'new-type' War Office Selection Board had been set up. The methods worked out here were adopted by other new boards, a dozen of which were started in various parts of the country by October 1942. A.T.S. Officer Selection Boards followed in 1943. Later, boards, on the same lines, were attached to Armies in the Middle East, India, Italy, and Western Europe. By the end of the war some 140,000 candidates had been through the new procedure of whom about 60,000 passed. (Vernon and Parry, 1949, p. 53.)

As many descriptions are available of the procedures carried out by these War Office Selection Boards (which have given their name to the W.O.S.B. technique), only a brief account is warranted here to emphasize important innovations. (Sutherland and Fitzpatrick, 1945; Garforth, 1945; Heard, 1946; Morris, 1949; Mercer, 1945; Bion, 1946; Harris, 1949; Rodger, 1948.)

The general procedure was to assemble candidates recommended for consideration at a centralized testing unit, which, under ideal circumstances, consisted of a 'guest-house' at which the selection staff and candidates lived and worked for a period of three to five days. Most Boards dealt with 64 to 120 candidates a week, divided up into groups of eight to ten. Each Board consisted of:

(i) a president—a senior army officer of wide military experience;

(ii) a vice-president;

(iii) one or more psychiatrists;

(iv) one or more psychologists;

(v) one or more military testing officers—with combat experience;

(vi) one or more sergeant testers.

These specialists were divided into teams who dealt with the respective groups of candidates passing through the testing centre. The candidates were anonymous and stripped of all insignia and outward means of identification. An informal atmosphere prevailed at the Board and military restrictions were reduced to a minimum. Observers mixed freely with the groups when testing was not actually in progress, and every opportunity was provided for obtaining an intimate knowledge of each candidate.

Vernon and Parry (1949, p. 59) list the main objects of the Boards as being to select candidates who would:

(i) Pass their O.C.T.U. courses and acquire the necessary technical proficiency.

(ii) Stand up well to the stresses of battle, showing resource, leadership, aggressiveness and caution when these qualities were needed.

(iii) Look after his men well and gain their confidence.

(iv) Co-operate effectively with other officers and make a good impression on his seniors.

To arrive at an assessment of the extent to which candidates were likely to measure up to these demands, the following types of test procedure were applied:

(i) Biographical data sheet;

(ii) Pencil-and-Paper Tests of general and specific mental abilities;

(iii) Personality Projection Tests, e.g. word association, thematic apperception, self-descriptions, etc.;

(iv) Individual practical assignments;

(v) Leaderless Group Tests:
   (a) Verbal—group discussions;
   (b) Performance—practical assignments;

(vi) Group-Leadership Tests (command situations):
   (a) Verbal—Chairman of Group Discussions;
   (b) Performance—practical assignments;

(vii) Psychiatric and psychological clinical interviews;

(viii) Final Board interview and assessment.

The most spectacular innovations in this testing programme were the group tests (known to-day as socio-dramatic or social-interaction tests), for the introduction of which Major W. R. Bion of the Royal Army Medical

Corps was largely responsible. Eaton (1947, p. 524) has succinctly defined the rationale of these tests as follows:

> Briefly, this hypothesis notes that it is useful (and particularly significant in a democratic society) to look upon the phenomenon of leadership as a *social value* and not merely as a psychological trait. To most psychologists, leadership denotes a complex pattern of individual behaviour tendencies such as 'intelligence', 'extroversion'. . . . They assume that there is a general quality of leadership. On the basis of this they proceed with the administration of individual psychological tests to spot these leader-personalities.

> This view neglects the fact that qualifications for leadership vary for different positions. The individual behaviour patterns that will be given recognition as indexes of leadership ability are not the same in a church, an army, a golf club, a labour union. . . . Leadership is a situationally defined capacity. The social values of the group—its objectives, interests, standards and mores—play an important part in determining what kind of personalities will be chosen for leadership. . . .

> These considerations form the theoretical basis for the claim that sociological techniques of leadership selection may have a higher potential validity than psychological tests. . . . It is in the light of this hypothesis that the socio-dramatic and sociometric experiments in leadership testing take on significance. . . .

> Socio-dramatic performance tests involve activity by an individual or group in a social situation of simulated reality.

> Sociometric measurements involve ratings of individuals by their co-workers, inferiors and/or superiors.

The application of group tests of the social-interaction type rests therefore on the assumption that these techniques create a real-life situation in which the individual can react spontaneously, and, in doing so, reveal temperamental, personality and character attributes of which he himself is perhaps unconscious. The trained observer can note the individuals' reactions and interpret them in relation to the total social situation in order to formulate conclusions regarding personality make-up, and the extent to which this is likely to make for effective leadership in the occupational field simulated in the test situation. Such an assessment, based on the combined judgements of observers with background knowledge and experience, was considered to be far more reliable and meaningful than, for example, that based on personality inventories of the questionnaire type.

As none of the above selection procedures had been validated the method of assessing candidates' potentialities in this field had to be undertaken on a subjective basis. This was done at a final conference of the Board at which all staff were present, and where the information on each candidate, culled from all sources, was made available in synoptic form. In general, and particularly in the final stages the conference procedures were standardized in terms of three phases:

(i) By a consideration of the life history, unit reports, interview reports by psychiatrist and president, military testing officers' description, etc., a general overall picture of the personality was obtained.

(ii) The next phase comprised the drawing up of a general conference profile. For this purpose two blackboards were used on which were recorded the assessors' ratings, and test results from all situations. Whenever there was disagreement evidence was called for so that a final judgement could be made.

(iii) When divergencies had been ironed out the agreed profile was considered and the candidate's final disposal was determined.

The list of items making up the profile was as follows:

(1) Leadership experience
(2) Unit report

(3) Officer intelligence rating
(4) Educational suitability
(5) Planning ability

(6) Practical ability
(7) Athletic ability

(8) Level of aims
(9) Effectiveness in pursuit of aims
(10) Military compatibility
(11) Sense of responsibility
(12) Social interest

(13) Quality of personal relations
(14) Range of personal relations
(15) Dominance
(16) Liveliness

(17) Stability of health

For obvious reasons, validation of this new technique could not be made on the classical lines of a follow-up study based on an unrestricted sample of candidates. However, indications of the early success of the W.O.S.B. methods came from other sources (W.O.S.B. Technical Memos. 1942, 1943, 1944). These findings were of a rather tentative nature, and do not warrant detailed mention here. They do, however, suggest:

(i) that the cadets selected by the New Type Boards appeared to be rated higher in training units than were those from the Old Type Boards, thereby diminishing the proportion of cadets rated below average;

(ii) that this achievement seemed to be effected without reducing the proportion of candidates selected;

(iii) that by focusing attention on officer selection, and by appealing to the sense of fairness of candidates, the new procedure seemed to play a part in increasing the supply of material;

(iv) that this combination of increased supply, and more efficient selection appeared to result in an increase in the number of above-average cadets sent to O.C.T.U. each month.

While no conclusive evidence is available to prove the above statements, the indications of success were sufficiently strong in favour of the New Type Selection Boards to encourage their continued adoption and wider application.

In a special edition of the *Review of Educational Research*, Sisson (1948) gives a synoptic review of the work undertaken by Personnel Research Sections of the Adjutant-General's Office established in America in 1940. Among the general problems of army classification and selection, he deals with the American attempts at selection of officer personnel. These procedures started in 1941 with the use of two forms of the Higher Examination containing vocabulary and arithmetic items. These were found to have lower predictive capacity of success at Officer Candidate Schools than did the Army General Classification Test (A.G.C.T.). Experiments were then made with two forms of Officer Candidate Tests (O.C.T. 1 and 2), which were first rejected. Later forms of the same type were reconstructed which had higher validity than the A.G.C.T. It is to be noted that these attempts concentrated exclusively on assessment of ability in terms of pencil-and-paper tests—no attempts were made to assess leadership qualities along the lines developed by W.O.S.B.

In October 1943 Murray and Stein (1943) were still lamenting the fact that no procedures similar to the W.O.S.B., which had been initiated in the British Army, and evidently also in the Canadian (though no reference is given), had yet been introduced in the American Army. The authors describe a schedule of tests (lasting a minimum of one hour) which they had tried out on small groups of R.O.T.C. (Army and Navy). No factual results are given, however, of the correlations between test assessments and commanding officers' ratings.

This gap was not long in being filled. In a book published by the Office of Strategic Services (O.S.S.) Assessment Staff (1948, p. 4 et seq.) a descriptive account is given as to how selection procedures of this type were introduced in America after October 1943. This is followed by an outline of the nature of the task confronting the O.S.S. staff and a comprehensive statement as to how they set about dealing with it. A briefer statement of the test procedures themselves has been given by Eaton (1947) and Murray and MacKinnon (1946). In general the O.S.S. assessment programme is essentially the same as the W.O.S.B.'s as is seen by the list of traits on which the candidates' profiles were drawn up:

(i) Motivation for O.S.S. service overseas.

(ii) Energy and zest.

(iii) Emotional stability.

(iv) Social relations.

(v) Leadership.

(vi) Ability to keep secret information.

(vii) Power of observation.

   (viii) Physical abilities.

    (ix) Practical intelligence in dealing with people, ideas, and things.

    (x) Ability to do effective propaganda.

The selection problems with which O.S.S. staff had to deal were of the same kind, although intensified in many ways. Thus the fields of employment for which they were required to predict success were perhaps more varied and unrelated when compared with the arms of the service in which officer personnel were to be employed after selection by W.O.S.B. Furthermore the O.S.S. assessment staff had far less information regarding the circumstances in which an individual would be operating in overseas duties. Consequently, in the O.S.S. assessment programme, especially at first where they were required to assess suitability for a particular overseas assignment, one finds many interesting variations of the theme of the socio-dramatic tests, e.g. stress interview, impromptu test situations and tests of frustration (snafu) tolerance. These indicate that the versatility of the sociological approach to the assessment of men is virtually unlimited, though considerable research will be necessary before our use of the procedures can be substantiated in terms other than their face-validity.

Because of manifold difficulties, and because it was ascertained later that individuals were assigned to jobs for which they had not been assessed, the O.S.S. staff decided that they would not only assess each man in relation to their conception of his designated assignment, but also 'in relation to nine large job categories as well'. The O.S.S. Assessment Board conducted its procedures in much the same way as did W.O.S.B. Thus, Murray and MacKinnon (1946, p. 79) state:

> Material from all these sources, interpreted in the light of the picture of the man obtained in the personal history interview, and, in turn, correcting that picture, was utilized in writing the Evaluation Note on the candidate which constituted the main part of the S Final Report. In this note of six to seven hundred words an attempt was made to convey in non-technical terms the main features of the character structure of the candidate.
>
> As the second part of the Final Report consisted of ratings on a six-point scale . . . of ten variables of personality, the first seven of which were considered important for all candidates, the last three of which were necessary for certain types of assignment. . . .
>
> This (the procedure) provided that the ratings of all personality variables of each candidate rated in a situation was the result of at least three independent ratings combined with final ratings in sub-staff conferences in which the performance of each candidate and its meaning were discussed at some length. . . .
>
> When the final form of the Evaluation Note had been agreed to by the staff as a whole, the final ratings of the variables for this candidate were made and a decision reached as to his suitability for his proposed assignment (i.e. Job Fitness Rating).

In addition to the O.S.S. experiment in America the Personnel Research Section of the Adjutant-General's Office has for some time been developing procedures for the selection of officers in the Regular United States Army.

It is not entirely clear how this work started and one can only infer from the literature that it succeeded the inauguration of O.S.S. procedures. The precise details of the testing programme are not available to the present author in that the reports of the Personnel Research Section quoted in Sisson's (1948) copious bibliography, when not classified for military security, may only be examined by qualified professional personnel by appointment in the office of the Personnel Research and Procedures Branch, the Adjutant-General's Office, Room AC 935, The Pentagon, Washington 25, D.C. Eaton's (1947) and Sisson's (1946) brief account of the project would seem to indicate that the procedures used involved W.O.S.B. techniques. The former (p. 533) states: 'Three of the classification tools, a General Survey Test, a Biographical Information Blank and Superior Officers Evaluation Reports are paper-pencil instruments. The fourth is a standardized socio-dramatic interview of each applicant by a board of trained officers to test a candidate's ability in dealing with people.'

These then were the most significant developments which took place during World War II in testing and selecting personnel for leadership and high-level or special assignments. The application of these techniques to the selection of executive and administrative staff in industry and public service organizations was fairly obvious and did not escape the notice of industrial psychologists operating in these fields. The most noteworthy and thorough-going application of W.O.S.B. techniques is undoubtedly that undertaken by the British Civil Service Commission in its attempts to fill the vacancies created by the war in the administrative class of its Civil and Foreign Service. For obvious practical reasons the basis of selection employed in times of peace—a highly academic competitive examination followed by an interview—could not legitimately be applied to ex-army candidates and temporary officers of the Service who had not had the opportunity to acquire the necessary knowledge and academic qualifications. Faced with this problem it was decided, in addition to a qualifying examination designed to test the quality rather than the content of a candidate's mind, to adopt the technique developed by the W.O.S.B.— viz. the institution of a Selection Board on residential lines. The main difference was that, unlike the W.O.S.B.s, this board had no powers of selection or rejection. It made its recommendations, in terms of results based on a three-day testing procedure, to the Final Selection Board set up by the Civil Service Commission. The procedures adopted by the C.I.S.S.B. staff and applied to all candidates who had passed the Qualifying Examination, have already been adequately listed and described by previous authors (Wilson, 1948; Vernon, 1950). From these accounts it will be seen that, allowing for suitable modifications to meet specific requirements, the psychological approach, test procedures used and method of assessment were essentially the same as those previously described for the W.O.S.B. and O.S.S. programmes.

The writer does not altogether agree with Vernon and Parry (1949, p. 64) when they state that: 'Group discussions, planning problems and the like are applied, though with the object of throwing light more on the quality or calibre of the candidates' intellectual powers than on their social adjustments.' As the result of fairly comprehensive job-analyses the fundamental requirements in a higher civil servant may be summarized as follows, which clearly indicates the importance attached to personality qualifications (Biesheuvel, 1945)*:

(a) A mind of first-rate quality, capable of dealing with policy in all its aspects: sensitive enough to recognize the emergence of a problem in its early stages—wide-ranging enough to see it, not only in its immediate, but in its widest setting—sufficiently creative to find the best possible solution and with the imagination to visualize its ultimate effects.

(b) The ability to analyse figures, reports or lengthy documents and to extract and summarize the essentials, to be able to write clear and acceptable minutes and letters. All this is paper work—backroom work of a higher secretarial nature.

(c) The faculty for effective personal contact; whether it is in informal discussion or in a difficult negotiation; as a member of a committee or as a speaker at a Conference. As the government takes more and more control into its hands, so the importance of this aspect increases—not only must the civil servant of to-day have to deal with other Government Departments or local Government officials, but he must be prepared to hold his own with business directors and organized labour, and to gain their confidence and respect.

Furthermore the type of individual report on each candidate under the headings listed below did give due prominence to personality and character attributes, viz.:

(i) Cognitive tests.

(ii) Group discussions.

(iii) Island story (written report).

(iv) Committee work (group discussion).

(v) In the chair (group leadership).

(vi) Short talk.

(vii) 'Seeded' group discussion.

(viii) Interviews by chairman, observer, and psychologist.

Credit for initiating the W.O.S.B. technique in the industrial field must go to Munro Fraser of the staff of the N.I.I.P. (1946, 1947, 1950). The first article gives a brief sketch of the procedures altered to suit industrial conditions and to fit into a testing programme of one day. The second contribution describes a more detailed programme and method of assessment covering one and a half days. His final communication in 1950 deals with a subjective evaluation of follow-up data covering some fifty New-Type Selection Boards carried out for various appointments in industry, together with some interesting suggestions for assessing performance in the group discussions.

* Since preparing this work for printing, a more detailed statement of the job requirements has been published in *Memorandum by the Civil Service Commissioners on the use of the Civil Service Selection Board in the Reconstruction Competitions.* H.M. Stationery Office, 1951, p.8.

Since the early post-war period the application of the W.O.S.B. technique has spread even further in the industrial field, and has even been applied in other spheres where leadership and other personality qualities are considered important. (Bridger and Isdell-Carpenter, 1947; Roff, 1948; Hoovers, 1948, and Beverstock, 1949.)

In the preceding paragraphs a brief outline has been given of the historical development of new techniques for the selection of individuals for leadership roles in a democratic society. The more spectacular innovations have been highlighted, for the purpose of placing the present research findings in their true perspective. In these large-scale experiments, psychological practice has run ahead of theory because of the urgency of the problems which had to be dealt with. It is significant that in the various Selection Boards set up, whether at W.O.S.B., O.S.S. or C.I.S.S.B., there were to be found working side by side psychologists of different schools of thought, and yet their specialized approach did not prevent them dealing with the practical assignments on an eclectic basis. No doubt at the time there would have been considerable differences in opinion as to the interpretation of candidates' test performance, behaviour and personality make-up, had there been time to sit back and indulge in theoretical discussions. The fact that co-operation on such a large scale was possible would seem to indicate that the theories of the different schools of thought will undergo considerable change, when psychologists and psychiatrists can study the material which has come to hand and record their own experiences and impressions while acting as members of the assessment teams, and it can possibly be expected that the independent systematologies will no longer be so insular in their approach to the study of behaviour as they were in the past. The most significant effect of this work will perhaps be this result, together with the fact that psychological doctrine will in the future have as its starting point the study of individuals falling within the wider range of normality, rather than the case histories of those seeking psychiatric advice and treatment.

A stage has now been reached where the psychologist must substantiate the use of these testing procedures by

(a) formulating adequate psychological theory to explain the observations and findings of these experiments;

(b) instituting further experiments on properly controlled lines to test these hypotheses and fill in the gaps in our knowledge.

Attempts to validate the tests by means of follow-up procedures were made during and at the end of the war, but they were greatly handicapped by the fact:

(i) that all groups studied were truncated by the process of selection and all results have to be corrected for restriction in the range of the samples;

(ii) that the occupational fields in which selected candidates were subsequently employed were so varied and changeable that the problem of obtaining consistent criteria was almost insuperable. This fact invariably had the unfortunate effect of reducing the size of samples studied to very meagre proportions.

There were other difficulties which have been fully dealt with by Vernon and Parry (1949, pp. 122-3), and the O.S.S. staff (1948, pp. 392–7).

What evidence of success of these techniques have we available to date, and what conclusions can be drawn from it within the limitations of these restricting conditions?

With the exception of one book (O.S.S. 1948) the research findings are only to be found in regard to W.O.S.B., O.S.S., and C.I.S.S.B., in short chapters of books or highly condensed articles in journals. It is appreciated that much analytical work has still to be carried out and that research findings may have been more comprehensively reported in secret document form, but it is also to be regretted that the results which have so far been made available have been so badly reported that a proper study cannot yet be attempted and one can only draw fairly tentative conclusions. These statements will be justified as we proceed to examine the evidence.

The only validation results which are available on the W.O.S.B.s (other than those previously mentioned in this chapter) are to be found in Morris (1949), Vernon and Parry (1949), and Reeve (1949). The findings can be conveniently reported under two main headings:—

(a) Comparative Studies between the Results of Old- and New-Type Selection Board Procedures

In regard to the demonstrable (as opposed to the assumed) success which these procedures have had in the past, the recent controversy between Morris (1949, 1950) and Ungerson (1950) raises many important issues. Morris (1949, p. 5) concedes the necessity for a validation study along proper lines, indicates why this was not possible in the case of W.O.S.B., and then suggests that we make an evaluation along different lines by considering firstly two questions:

(i) How satisfactory, in general, was the performance in officer roles of candidates selected by W.O.S.B. methods?

(ii) How far did W.O.S.B.s satisfy the expectancies and needs of the army and civilian communities, including the officer candidates themselves?

In reply to these Morris (1949, p. 6) states that: 'In follow-up studies in the Mediterranean Campaign (1943–4) it was found that in the opinion of commanding officers 76% of officers selected by W.O.S.B. methods were giving completely satisfactory service.' He does not give us figures for the Old-Type Boards, which should be used as a basis for comparison and experimental control, and proceeds to argue that 'this does not mean that no control exists and that these results cannot be evaluated'. He then claims (p. 7) that: 'In fact a control does operate, only it is implicit, inexact and largely unconscious, and this is shown by the fact that a selection procedure is only socially tolerated if its efficiency rises above a certain limit, which, however difficult to specify, clearly does exist. It was ultimately, of course, because the efficiency of Old Procedure Boards fell below this limit that they were replaced by W.O.S.B.s. Comparisons in such cases are implicitly made with an existing social norm whose meaning is definable in terms of social necessity.'

The objection to this argument is that what will or will not be 'tolerated' depends very much on the 'norm' of the social group which has the whip hand or authority to decide. Furthermore, it is doubtful whether the yardstick used when reaching a decision of this type is the scientific efficiency of the system, and not its 'efficiency' in the satisfaction or promotion of the vested interests of the group concerned. Finally, Morris has not described how efficiency is to be assessed when two social norms are in conflict with each other. The answer to this one must, in terms of the 'implicit, inexact and unconscious controls', approach very nearly to the doctrine of 'might is right' and smacks of those political theories where all actions are justified 'in the name of the state'. These comments become even more significant in the light of Morris's footnote (1949, p. 7) in which he admits:

> . . . no strict comparison can be made between officers selected by W.O.S.B.s and those selected by Old Procedure Boards (Simple Interview Boards). In the Mediterranean Campaign the 'satisfaction rate' for Old Procedure Officers was of the same order—slightly but not significantly lower—as for W.O.S.B.s, but the majority of these officers were passed by Old Procedure Boards before W.O.S.B.s came into being. For the period of common operation of the two systems, the difference is statistically, of borderline significance, in favour of W.O.S.B.s.

We would agree with Morris that the first two questions 'are not concerned with explicit and exact comparisons, nor with predictions'. We would agree also that facts of experience are none the less facts to be taken into account with evidence from other sources, and we would agree in theory that social norms, levels of social tolerance and thresholds of security are legitimate concepts; but we would resolutely stand our ground in asserting that until the techniques and skills for dealing with social phenomena have been perfected to the stage where 'social norms', 'thresholds' and other as yet vaguely defined concepts have been pinned down in terms of rigorous definitions which can be applied by all in a consistent manner, he has not demonstrated to us that the facts of experience in the present case are anything other than 'private matters' which carry no weight in scientific validation. Consequently until such time as the necessary conditions have been satisfied, we have no other alternative but to fall back on the existing means at our disposal and in this respect we must agree with Ungerson (1950) that 'if we do not validate strictly, then we can only offer psychologists' opinions against laymen's opinions. If, on the other hand, we accept the restricted and more usual definition of evaluation, then we should, in time, reach the situation in which we can confront laymen's opinions with the scientific facts.' Consequently it is along these lines that an attempt will be made here to evaluate the success which can be claimed for these procedures.

In the light of these comments a 'satisfaction rate' of 76% cannot be regarded as 'a matter for congratulation', until it can be established that (a) this rate is significantly greater than could be produced on the basis of pure chance selection and (b) that this significant improvement over chance yields gains (in terms of reduced training wastage and increased number of capable personnel) which exceed losses (in terms of increased cost of selection, loss of time, etc.). When considering these questions it should not be forgotten that selection by 'chance' never produces a complete crop of 'failures' or even that the failure-success ratio will be 50–50. The failure-success ratio in the randomly selected group will always equal the ratio of failure-success in the population from which the group is selected. In some instances, particularly in the case where the parent population is itself a selected one in terms of 'eligibility for consideration', it is possible that the percentage of failures in the eligible population is only 25%—in which case random selection would also result in 75% of the selectees being 'successful'. Thus until one knows where the success-failure dividing line lies in the parent population, it is impossible to say what improvement any newly devised selection procedure makes over chance, and whether this gain is sufficiently large to warrant its adoption in favour of the more economic device of spinning a coin. Consequently one cannot accept, without additional data, the 'satisfaction rate' quoted by Morris as sufficient justification of the W.O.S.B. procedures.

The next evidence which is produced (Morris, 1949, p. 8) is a little more encouraging and is represented in the following table:—

Table 1

Overall comparison between W.O.S.B. and Old Procedure cadets with respect to ratings of Officer Cadet Training Units (all O.C.T.U.s combined)

	Percentage rated			Total numbers
	Above average	*Average*	*Below average*	
W.O.S.B.	35	40	25	721
Old Procedure ..	22	41	37	491

In this case the proportion of candidates selected by W.O.S.B. and the Old Procedures, rated above and below average by the Training Authorities, is compared. When 'treated as a 3 by 2 table the two distributions are significantly different at the 1% level. Thus W.O.S.B.s not only significantly reduced the below average material but added significantly to the above average material.' (Morris, 1949, p. 8.) However, when the findings of the ten different O.C.T.U.s are reviewed, which are here combined, this desirable result was only true of four of them, but 'At no single O.C.T.U. was a significant difference found in favour of the Old Procedure' (p. 9). Morris appreciates that the type of material which was available at the time of operation of the New- and Old-Type Boards could have had an important bearing on these results, but assures us that 'examination of the sources of supply revealed no evidence which suggested that candidates going before the two types of Board were likely to differ in quality' (p. 9). As no supporting evidence is given for this statement, we can only deal with it as with any other personal assurance, and remain sceptical;

particularly as it is known (W.O.S.B., 1943) that the number of candidates becoming available for selection increased after the introduction of W.O.S.B. techniques.

A number of other comparative studies were also carried out but 'it proved impossible to get really satisfactory samples. Moreover, in no case was any clear difference found between W.O.S.B. and Old Procedure officers in general, in either direction. A number of specific differences in favour of W.O.S.B.s was found, but on the whole the evidence was conflicting and exceedingly difficult to evaluate. . . . In view of the sampling problems and other difficulties to be mentioned later, the only legitimate inference is not that there was no difference, but that the case for or against any such difference is not proven.' (Morris, 1949, p. 10.)

(b) Validation Study of W.O.S.B. Procedures against Criteria of Success

The method of reporting the results of studies of this type leaves much to be desired. Morris (1949) reports validity coefficients of the order of ·3 to ·35 between W.O.S.B. Final Grades, intelligence and other tests, and the O.C.T.U. training grades. Vernon and Parry (1949, p. 125) report that: 'A correlation of $+\cdot28$ (uncorrected for selectivity) was obtained between A.T.S., W.O.S.B. and O.C.T.U. gradings, but the agreement of W.O.S.B. with assessments of A.T.S. officers in their units, although positive, was very small.' They also report a correlation of ·165 (uncorrected), ·35 (corrected), between W.O.S.B. grades and Commanding Officers' assessments in a group of 500 infantry and artillery officers. In view of these small coefficients one is somewhat surprised that Vernon and Parry (1949) should have dealt so briefly with later studies where there is a considerable improvement in the magnitude of correlation. These findings are casually reported as follows (p. 125):

> In the post-war period, operational follow-up has been impossible. But a large [sic] number of investigations have proved that W.O.S.B. grades give fair predictions of success at O.C.T.U. Under *properly controlled conditions* [my own italics] correlations consistently reach the $+\cdot4$ to $+\cdot5$ level, though they depend greatly on the skill of the particular board members, and on the thoroughness of the O.C.T.U. assessments.

No further comments are made on this 'large number of investigations'. Stated in this form these findings cannot be properly evaluated. For example, can one assume that the 'properly controlled conditions' meant that the follow-up was conducted on a group which was not truncated by selection, and are the coefficients reported, therefore uncorrected? If this is not so, the fact should be clearly stated, together with other necessary information, since corrections of correlations can only be justified under certain specific conditions. Again Morris (1949, p. 11) quotes a 'correlation using six variables, including Final Grade, gave a figure of 0·58 with O.C.T.U. outcome', but regards this as 'not of much use for predictive purposes, since it accounts for about only one third of the variance of the criterion'. Again we are not advised as to whether the coefficient is a corrected or uncorrected one, nor of the formula used for this purpose—a vital piece of information in this case since one suspects that the basic assumptions in terms of which it is permissible to use the appropriate formula are not applicable to the data. Furthermore, his naïve reason (frequently used in psychological literature it is admitted) is insufficient to reject a correlation coefficient of this magnitude. It has been shown (Arbous, 1953) that under certain conditions where the dividing line between success and failure in the criterion is propitious, and where the battery cut-off score is suitably chosen, a test battery can render a useful service in selection, even when the correlation between it and the criterion is low. Thus with a validity coefficient for the test battery score of $r=\cdot6$ where the failure-success dividing line in the criterion indicates that approx. 25% of the population can be successful, and where the battery cut-off score is placed at 65 standard score, the test battery efficiency index (i.e. its gain over chance selection in the percentage of selectees who turn out to be successful) will be 47%. As these conditions may apply in the case of officer selection, where quality is being chosen for a high-level occupation, and where the consequences of failure are very serious, a gain of this magnitude cannot lightly be ignored.

Reeve (1949) reports a correlation of $\cdot58$ 'between the W.O.S.B. and O.C.T.U. gradings of 33 candidates who were successful at the O.C.T.U.' Can this be the same study referred to by Morris (1949)? The coefficient in this case is uncorrected and restriction has been affected in respect of both variables, the group being reduced by selection to about one-third of its original size. In view of this and the small number of cases the coefficient should be cautiously interpreted. However, the results are encouraging.

Chapter IX of the Assessment of Men (O.S.S. 1948, p. 392) gives an account of the O.S.S. Staff's attempt to evaluate their assessment procedures. They emphasize at the outset that,

> because O.S.S. urgently needed personnel to carry out its operations, in the early months of the work all energies had to be turned to the pressing requirements of selection; appraisal of the efficiency of the process had to be postponed. When at last it was possible to establish a comprehensive program of validation procedures, the unexpectedly rapid end of the war cut it short. These unfavourable circumstances added tremendously to the difficulty of our basic task: that of establishing satisfactory criteria by which to measure accuracy either of diagnoses of personality or of prognoses of performance in a specific assignment.
>
> These complexities bulked so large that we were unable to overcome them all. Although thousands of man-hours were spent in the evaluation process, the final verdict is a question mark. Nearly all the members of the staff and many of their colleagues in O.S.S. . . . had the strong impression that, by and large, the administration had been furnished with meaningful descriptions of the traits and abilities of the recruits, which were of considerable service in winnowing the wheat from the chaff, and in placing the wheat where it belonged. . . . Unhappily the final result was a decrease, rather than an increase, in degree of certainty—a temporarily discomforting but, in the long run, often productive state of mind.

In fairness to the O.S.S. staff the almost insuperable obstacles to a validation study should be borne in mind. These are dealt with in detail in the book, and the main difficulties can be summarized as follows:

(i) Job analyses were inadequate for assessment purposes. In assessing each candidate there was no clear picture in the minds of the staff of the duties which he would be required to perform. Assessments were therefore mostly in terms of all-round suitability, whereas in fact, in the operational theatre, he was more often required to cope only with a limited number of specific situations.

(ii) There was 'the very frequent occurrence of unpredictable changes in the jobs and in the environments to which men were assigned in the theater. Theoretically, the whole process of validation becomes meaningless under these circumstances:' (O.S.S., 1948, p. 394.)

(iii) 'One of the defects of the enterprise resulting from the requirements of the practical situation was that only a very few candidates who were not recommended by the assessment staff went overseas. Usually they left the organization.' (O.S.S., 1948, p. 396.)

Four separate criteria were established:

(i) *Overseas Staff Appraisal*

This assessment was undertaken by members of O.S.S. staff who conducted patterned interviews with the individual's immediate chief or commanding officer.

(ii) *Theatre Commander Appraisal*

'. . . when any member of the organization returned from an overseas assignment, his immediate superior submit a report including ratings on personality traits as soon as the individual left the theater.' (O.S.S. 1948, p. 399.)

(iii) *Reassignment Area Appraisal*

This consisted of a re-evaluation of personnel who had completed one tour of duty. Performance overseas was appraised in terms of (*a*) experience in the field; (*b*) developmental history; and (*c*) political and social attitudes.

(iv) *Returnee Appraisal*

During interview with Appraisal Area staff returning officers were requested to provide personality descriptions of fellow officers. These enabled assessments to be made as to how effective the latter had been in their duties overseas.

In view of the difficulties mentioned earlier it is not surprising that coefficients of agreement between the four criteria varied only between ·46 and ·59. The general and specific inadequacies of these criteria are comprehensively dealt with in the text together with an analysis of the appraisal populations which can be briefly summarized as follows:—

Table 2

Number appraised	Percentage of assessed persons going overseas	Criteria
511	19	Returnee appraisal
468	17	Theatre commander
466	17	Overseas staff
411	15	Reassignment area

There were of course many overlaps, some individuals being assessed by more than one method.

Since the O.S.S. staff found that 'the complete detailed analysis of these appraisal data is not of sufficient interest to justify publication', we can only report some of the major findings and conclusions here. These can be conveniently summarized in a table reproduced from the original text.

Table 3

Showing Validity Coefficients (corrected) for O.S.S. Assessments

Type of appraisal	S-Job rating (classes s-45 on)		W-Job rating (all classes)	
	r	N	r	N
Overseas staff appraisal	·37[a]	88	·53[a]	83
Returnee appraisal	·19[a]	93	·21[a]	173
Theatre commander appraisal ..	·23	64	·15	158
Reassignment area appraisal ..	·08	53	·30[a]	178

The 'r' given in each case is the corrected one, and cases in which correcting 'r' for restricted sample made a significant difference are denoted by 'a'. Three conclusions should be noted here:

(i) That the size of the samples studied has been considerably reduced by experimental factors.

(ii) That this, together with the manner in which the original population of candidates was truncated by the O.S.S. assessments, renders the application of correction formulae a very hazardous procedure. It cannot be known whether these factors will serve to underestimate or overestimate the true 'r'.

(iii) One has no confidence in evaluating the relative merits of the criteria in terms of these coefficients, for, as Thorndike has pointed out (1949, p. 170): 'this type of selection affects not only the absolute size of validity coefficients but also their relative size. . . .' Furthermore, even if the Overseas Staff Appraisal were the one yielding the highest validity, one suspects that spurious factors may enter the degree of correlation here.

One must agree, therefore, with the O.S.S. staff's own conclusion to the effect that the findings which are so far available are not very impressive, and it is difficult to decide whether this is due to one or more of the following:—

(i) The appraisal (i.e. criteria) procedures were defective.

(ii) The assessment procedures were defective.

(iii) The staff members were to some extent incompetent.

(iv) 'An individual's relative effectiveness under such shifting conditions as prevailed for O.S.S. men and women overseas depends more upon chance—the occurrence of improbable and unpredictable situations and events—than it does upon relative ability, degree of motivation, and strength of character.'

The courageous conclusions reached by the O.S.S. staff might well be quoted here because of their importance for future research workers (O.S.S., 1948, p. 448–9):

The recitation of our difficulties and failures, we hope, will stimulate others to concentrate on the problems of appraisal. This enterprise is more difficult than that of assessment, because the conditions under which appraisees operate are more varied and complex, less susceptible to formulation, and the performances of appraisees are likewise more varied and complex, and only a few segments of them are open to inspection. . . . An adequate system of appraisal must rest on clearly defined criteria of merit arrived at after an analysis of environments and jobs. The task calls for a thorough study of field conditions.

Since the criteria of appraisal define the standard against which the efficacy of assessment will be measured, they constitute the target of prediction. Therefore, we submit, the system of appraisal should be set up *before* the system of assessment.

The results of the work done by the Personnel Research Section of the Adjutant-General's Office in America appear to be more encouraging in the field of officer selection for the Regular Army. While these cannot be reviewed in detail for reasons already stated, Eaton's (1947) short resumé shows that the tests would have a combined multiple correlation of ·67 with the criterion. In this instance a large number of cases was used— 13,000, of whom 3,000 were involved in the validation study. ('1,000 officers were agreed to be *outstanding*, 1,000 were agreed to be *average*, and 1,000 were agreed to be *inferior*. The remaining 10,000 were not rated clearly and consistently by all raters and were not used in the study.') The criterion appeared to consist of a sociometric rating device by (i) a superior, (ii) an equal, and (iii) an inferior officer. Furthermore there would appear to be no truncation of the group studied. These results may have one limitation, viz. that prediction in terms of the tests may be confined to those individuals who can be consistently rated by the three types of assessors concerned, and hence may tell us little about those on whom there is disagreement, i.e. the 10,000.

The work done in this field by Beverstock (1949) is interesting, but deserves little attention in this study. Its main deficiencies can be listed as follows:

(i) The groups studied are very small: n=25, and n=15.

(ii) The groups are truncated by selection.

(iii) One criterion is suspect: the tests and rating results were balanced 'against the final overall assessment, since this is [*sic!*] at least the best estimate of potential success'.

(iv) 'The other criterion was composed of ratings made during the one-year course on academic work, discussion group activities, and practical ability shown in the Clubs.' Although only *one* of the assessors had been a member of the Selection Board, this information does not help us to evaluate the effect of this spurious factor without knowing how many there were altogether—this information is not supplied.

(v) Without giving the reader any indication as to how rank order correlations (based on a restricted sample of fifteen cases) between individual tests and the criterion are reduced to the form of multiple correlation coefficients one is at a loss as to how to interpret the latter figures given.

The only results to hand on the validity of the Civil Service Selection Board Procedures (C.I.S.S.B.) are those reported by Vernon (1950). It is to be regretted that this 'exceptionally important paper' could not have been produced at greater length, for as it stands in its highly condensed form, many research gaps are left unfilled particularly on controversial points which make it difficult to evaluate the results. This article gives very briefly a list of test procedures employed, a brief statement as to how C.I.S.S.B. gradings and the Final Selection Board assessments were made, followed by a factor analysis study of the structure of C.I.S.S.B. gradings for what this is worth. There is, however, space only for an evaluation of the follow-up investigations in the present study.

Five follow-up criteria were used:

(i) Selected officers were graded by one officer on a 5-point scale in terms of the ultimate rank which he expected the candidate to reach in the service. This officer was in charge of a fortnight's staff training course—whose judgement was said to have 'a high reputation'. (n=106)

(ii) 'A follow-up form was designed by C.I.S.S.B. staff and was explained by them to supervising officers in the Departments where the first 147 administrative candidates had been working for one year or over. This form asked for 5- or 6-point ratings on the 13 qualities . . . also for an overall grading, an estimate of probable final rank, and a free pen-picture.' (Vernon, 1950, p. 84.)

(iii) A similar follow-up form was applied to the first 55 candidates accepted for the Foreign Service.

(iv) A single grading of suitability was obtained from the head of the Foreign Office Personnel Department on these 55 candidates and on an additional 68. (n=123)

(v) 'At the end of their 2-year probation period, Administrative officers were reassessed on a (slightly revised) follow-up form.' (Vernon, 1950, p. 85.)

The validity coefficients for each of the tests in respect of each of the five criteria (where applicable) is then listed, together with corrected validities in respect of criteria (ii), (iv) and (v).

Of all the individual test variables and in respect of all the criteria, only four of the uncorrected validity coefficients are greater than ·3. These are the following:—

Table 4

	Validity coefficients —uncorrected	
	Criteria	
Test	i	iii
C.I.S.S.B. verbal test		·450
Observer's rating in committee		·307
Chairman's rating on individual problem		·356
Chairman's interview	·403	

In the Final C.I.S.S.B. grades, i.e. where the chairman, observer and psychologist reviewed all the test data to hand, and arrived at a final assessment, the only validity coefficients (uncorrected) which were as great as ·301 to ·456 were in respect of criterion (i)—the assessment by the training officer after a fortnight's training course. Apart from these results the majority of the uncorrected validity coefficients were of the order ·1 to ·2.

Some significant changes take place, however, after correction by the 'appropriate' formulae, and the validity coefficients of some tests rise, for example, from ·274 to ·507 for the psychologist's interview in respect of criterion (iv), ·048 to ·303 for the observer's rating on committee procedure (criterion ii), ·144 to ·476 from the chairman's interview against criterion (v), etc. In the final gradings the corrected and uncorrected validities can be compared as follows:—

Table 5

	Validity coefficients for Final Selection Board mark	
	Uncorrected	*Corrected*
Criterion 1	·456	·824
Criterion 2	·230	·504
Criterion 3	·387	·657
Criterion 4	·413	·617
Criterion 5	·287	·563

As this portion of the study, dealing with the techniques of correction, is the most crucial, it is regretted that it has not been dealt with by Vernon in a more detailed and rigorous manner. As far as can be ascertained (apart from correction for these variables subsumed under the Qualifying Examination) two types of correction were involved in this study. These will be examined with some care:

(a) 'The best plan appeared to be to apply univariate correction to the Final Selection Board (F.S.B.) mark alone.' Though the formula in this case is not given, we must assume that it is the one referred to in Thorndike's (1949,* p. 173) Case 2, i.e. when estimating the correlation between two variables 1 and 2, when an observed 'r' has been calculated on a sample which has been restricted in terms of one of the two variables. Correction by use of this formula is valid 'provided one can be sure of the tenability of two assumptions: that the regressions are linear and that the arrays are homoscedastic for the scatter based on the uncurtailed distribution' (McNemar, 1949, p. 126). A statement as to the tenability of these assumptions in this particular instance would have been welcome rather than to have made the 'customary assumption' that the conditions are satisfied in all cases. This is important, since it is known that these conditions are quite frequently violated by rating devices such as have been used in both F.S.B. mark and criteria.

(b) All other C.I.S.S.B. variables were corrected by use of the formula given in the text. Vernon omits to mention, however, that the use of this formula is only justifiable under certain conditions, and consequently does not examine to what extent these apply to the data. It becomes necessary, therefore, for the reader to do this for himself in order to evaluate the results. The effect of this is not very encouraging.

The same formula is quoted by Thorndike (1949, p. 174) when dealing with Case 3 as to the manner in which restriction of the sample has been affected. 'In this case we are still concerned with the correlation between variables 1 and 2. However, we are now dealing with a case in which curtailment has been neither upon variable 1 nor variable 2 but upon some third variable.' Of this formula Thorndike (1949, p. 175) makes the specific observations:

So far, we have limited our consideration to the situation in which restriction of the group has been carried out on a single score. It has been assumed that magnitude of score on this variable is the only consideration determining whether or not an applicant will be accepted. No other considerations enter into the decision in any way. In practice, this idealized situation often (perhaps generally) does not prevail. The actual situation may deviate from the simple pattern which we have outlined in either or both of two ways. First, selection

* Quotations from this source are reprinted by permission from *Personnel Selection: Test and Measurement Techniques* by R. L. Thorndike, published by John Wiley & Sons, Inc., 1949.

may have been based on specific reference to two or more scores. Second, selection may have been based on reference in unspecified and unspecifiable ways to various intangible and subjective factors which were never combined into a score. Of these two complications, the former represents a considerable increase in and complication of the statistical and computational labors of correcting the obtained values; the second represents an insuperable obstacle to any analytical treatment. When selection is based, as it often is, on a clinical judgment which combines in an unspecified and inconstant fashion various types of data about the applicant, and when this judgment is not expressed in any type of quantitative score, one is at a loss as to how to estimate the extent to which the validity coefficient for any test procedure has been affected by that screening.

In the present instance Vernon is correcting the correlations between any C.I.S.S.B. test variable and the criteria, when curtailment of the group has been affected by the F.S.B. mark. Let us now examine how the restriction of the sample in this manner 'deviates from the simple pattern' required by the correction formula, with particular reference to the 'two ways' mentioned by Thorndike above.

(i) *Where selection is based on reference to two or more scores*

Vernon states that the Final Selection Board 'alone decided which candidates should be accepted or rejected'. However in doing so it re-interviewed each candidate and was also largely guided by the overall C.I.S.S.B. grade and final report. However, the Final Selection Board 'often modified the final (i.e. published) marks'.

In this case selection is really being effected in terms of

(a)   the interview assessment of the F.S.B.;

(b)   the overall C.I.S.S.B. grade and final report.

It should be noted, moreover, that the C.I.S.S.B. grade, in turn, is based on the average of the three gradings of the chairman, observer and psychologist, all of whom have carefully studied the test information of candidates from all sources, and who have each interviewed the candidate personally.

Clearly selection of the sample in this case was effected in terms not only of two, but a whole host of variables combined in an indefinable and inconsistent manner.

(ii) *Where selection is based on reference in an unspecifiable way to subjective factors which were never combined into a score*

From the above it will be clear that the F.S. Board in its interview with each candidate, though guided by the C.I.S.S.B. grading, was not bound by it and 'often modified the final marks'. The F.S.B. apparently did not rate candidates on their interview alone independently of the C.I.S.S.B. grading, and then combine the two arithmetically. Clearly the candidate's F.S.B. mark was based 'on reference in unspecifiable ways to various intangible and subjective factors (in the minds of the F.S.B.) which were never expressed in any type of quantitative score'.

The application of the correction formula to the data before us would, therefore, appear to be unpermissible on both counts. Our confidence in the resulting corrected validity coefficients is consequently shaken, though in fairness to the author it must be stated that one does not know whether the use of the formula in the present case has served to overestimate or underestimate the true coefficients. In view of the above considerations one should be cautious in interpreting the claim that 'the writer has not come across any others (validity coefficients) superior to these in the literature of high-grade selection'.

A review of the work done in this field leads one to an appreciation of the manifold difficulties which beset the path of the research worker, and of the enormous amount of spadework which has still to be done. One is to-day still forced to the conclusion reached by the O.S.S. staff in respect of their own attempt (O.S.S., 1948, p. 393):

> The negative statistical outcome would probably have deterred us from the huge labour of this book if it had shaken our faith in the general principles underlying the O.S.S. system of assessment and if we had not firmly believed that we had succeeded in distinguishing most of the defects in our implementation of the system. Anyhow, it is clear that the picture presented in this volume is not that of a noble building ready for occupancy, but rather a mass of rubble with many good blocks of granite and marble out of which a substantial edifice can be erected in the future. This chapter, with its emphasis upon our errors, may prove more useful than any other in the book, especially if the reader pays close attention to the defects in our validation procedures and employs his imagination in thinking of ways to rectify them.

In the light of these comments we shall proceed, with due caution, to report our attempt to make something of the 'blocks of granite and marble' bequeathed by predecessors working in this field.

CHAPTER II

PROBLEMS TO BE FACED

In DECIDING ON suitable selection procedures to meet the requirements of the scheme, the N.I.P.R. was faced with the following technical problems and practical considerations:

(1) Candidates had to be selected, not for a specific well-defined job, but for the wide, ill-defined field of high-level administrative work.

(2) By virtue of the nature of the scheme, the main task was that of selecting candidates of high potential ability and adaptability, who would be likely to measure up to the exacting demands of the training period and prove capable of leadership *in the future*. With younger candidates particularly, this involved the assessment of capacity for future development and maturation—a difficult task.

(3) For practical considerations candidates could only be made available for testing and assessment procedures for a limited period of time.

(4) A highly concentrated programme of testing would make heavy demands on the N.I.P.R. staff available; many of whom would have to be taken off other research projects to carry out this programme.

(5) An adequate job analysis of the requirements of administrative work in the organization was not available. Despite this, however, decisions had to be made on the abilities and qualities required by the candidates for success as trainees.

(6) The possibility of measuring these abilities and qualities adequately with the test material and procedures immediately available had to be considered. Procedures for the selection of high-level administrative workers had not previously been standardized either in South Africa or overseas. Consequently where tests were lacking for this project, new ones had to be devised.

It is necessary to deal with some of these points in detail as they were decisive factors in determining the nature of the whole selection programme.

(1) *The time available for testing*

In the initial discussions with the Corporation's representatives it was decided that a committee should go through all written applications and select a limited number of candidates to be put through the N.I.P.R. selection procedures. The testing programme was, therefore, designed to deal with this limited number of candidates, and allowed sufficient time to put each candidate through a very thorough series of tests. At a later date, however, the Management Board decided, for reasons of internal policy, that it was advisable to give all internal applicants a chance to go through the selection procedures. The N.I.P.R. was thus approached at the last minute, with a request to revise its programme to meet this change in policy. This was agreed to, although it was pointed out that testing a greatly increased number of candidates would throw a considerable strain on the limited number of N.I.P.R. personnel available, and would necessitate the speeding up of selection procedures. In particular it would involve the shortening of the clinical interview with each candidate from one hour to half an hour; a rather inadequate period of time for a key test in the selection programme. It was regarded as impracticable to ask candidates to make themselves available for testing for a period longer than two days.

(2) *Availability of N.I.P.R. staff*

To compensate for the lack of standardized test procedures, and because, in any case, many of the important qualities desired could not be measured in quantitative terms, but depended upon the judgements of assessors, it was felt that the most experienced members of the N.I.P.R. staff should be made available for the programme. These members of staff had to be taken off their own research projects and other outside commitments. This was practicable for a limited period, and would have been possible to meet the demands of the programme as *originally* planned. However, the decision that all internal applicants should be tested meant in the end that some 240 candidates had to pass through the test. Clearly the other commitments of the N.I.P.R. staff could not be left unattended for the period of time required for this additional task. The result was inevitably that the programme itself had to be curtailed.

(3) *The nature of abilities and qualities required*

On the basis of (*a*) a theoretical analysis of the requirements of high-level administrative work, and (*b*) the experience collected in England during the war in the selection of officers, and later, in the selection of Civil Service personnel, it was decided that the following qualities were desirable in successful candidates:

(*a*) Superior, or at least above-average, all-round mental ability.

(*b*) Satisfactory *curriculum vitae* and educational background.

(*c*) Evidence of an alive interest in, and knowledge of current affairs and matters of national importance.

(*d*) Keen occupational interest in administrative work, and good motivation for it.

(*e*) Ability to handle people satisfactorily in interpersonal situations.

(*f*) Ability to weigh up and assess people, particularly in relation to work demands.

(*g*) Ability to establish good working relations with colleagues.

(*h*) Actual or potential leadership qualities.

(i) Planning and organizing ability, i.e. the ability to grasp essentials, think through a problem logically and marshal facts in support of conclusions.

(j) Possession of an alert and pleasing personality make-up, with good presence.

(k) A fairly high degree of ambition and the necessary drive to achieve success.

(l) Adaptability.

(m) Physical stamina.

(n) A high degree of personal integrity.

(o) A stable, well-integrated personality, i.e. free from traits of emotional instability and feelings of personal insecurity and inadequacy.

It was felt that administrative trainees should measure up to all or most of these demands adequately. In view of the fact that the selected candidates would be regarded by existing employees of the corporation in a very critical light, and demands would be made on their character and personality make-up, over and above those normally required by their work, it was felt that a very high standard should be set for acceptance. The success of the whole venture would depend to a large extent on the degree to which the pioneer group of candidates won 'acceptance' for themselves from the existing administrative body. Consequently it was decided that, where candidates showed serious deficiencies in any of the above qualities, they should not be recommended for acceptance.

(4) *Test procedures available*

Though no procedure for selecting high-level administrative staff in industry had previously been standardized and validated at the time, there was, fortunately, one technique closely related to the selection task set by the Trainee Scheme, viz. those which have been described in the previous chapter. The main purpose of the C.I.S.S.B. tests is to select candidates for the Administrative Division of the British Civil Service. An extremely high standard is set, and the emphasis is on high all-round ability, backed by the requisite personality, temperament and character qualities. These were essentially the same qualities as those required by the present Trainee Scheme. It was decided, therefore, that a modified version of the C.I.S.S.B. procedures, suitably adapted to allow for local and industrial requirements, would be the best available to use in the selection of administrative trainees. This decision was, moreover, influenced by the fact that the N.I.P.R. had already made use of these testing methods in selecting officer personnel for the Union Defence Force, and also officials in senior administrative posts in local commercial and industrial organizations. Members of the N.I.P.R. staff were thus familiar with these techniques. It was against this background, therefore, that the test battery, described in the following pages, was finally chosen.

CHAPTER III

DESCRIPTION OF TESTS

THE FINAL TEST BATTERY comprised fifteen different test situations, which, for convenience of description, are grouped as follows:

(1) Information on candidate's life and background.
(2) Objective tests of general and specific mental abilities.
(3) Tests of behaviour in interpersonal situations of an intimate nature.
(4) Tests of behaviour in group-test situations.
(5) Tests of ability to deal with administrative problems on paper.
(6) Relationships with colleagues.
(7) Projection tests of personality.
(8) Clinical interview assessment.

The test descriptions which follow are intended to give a general picture of the procedures which each candidate passed through, and to indicate the manner in which each candidate's score or assessment was obtained.

(1) *Information on Candidate's Background*

(a) Biographical inventory

This is a 15-page inventory, designed to elicit from the candidate the necessary information on his life and background. It is not a test. The candidate is given adequate time in which to complete it, and is free to answer the questions in any manner he may choose. Broadly, the questions cover home, educational and occupational background, leisure and sporting interests, personal habits and preferences, and health. A check on the information supplied by the candidate is made during the clinical interview.

(b) General knowledge test

This is a test consisting of a number of questions on the political, economic, scientific, and cultural life of South Africa and the world in general. The main object of the test is to measure (i) the spread of the candidate's general knowledge, and (ii) the extensiveness of knowledge in any given area. The test is specifically designed for adults who have spent most of their lives in South Africa, and as a result, recent arrivals from overseas were at a disadvantage in completing it.

It is doubtful whether a test of this nature could ever be adequately standardized owing to the fact that norms would soon become out of date. In its present form it did enable the psychologist conducting the clinical interview to arrive at a subjective assessment of the breadth of a candidate's interest in national and international affairs. This evaluation could then be incorporated in the overall estimate of the individual's suitability as an administrative trainee.

(c) *The clinical interview*

The most important information on the candidate's life is obtained from the clinical interview, but this situation will be described more fully later.

(2) *Objective Tests of Mental Abilities*

These tests are vital to the test battery. They are designed to test various aspects of individual mental ability, and have been adequately standardized. They were used extensively in the South African Air Force during the war for the selection of air crew personnel, and norms have been calculated on a representative sample of the adult European population with an educational standard of Junior Certificate and above (including university graduates). The tests are completely objective in the sense that all answers are either right or wrong, and the influence of the examiner on results is nil.

In the present battery four tests were used:

(a) *Test A (F)*

This is an adaptation made by the Aptitude Test Section of the South African Air Force, of the Otis Group Intelligence Test. It consists of 65 items, and the candidate is allowed 35 minutes for completion.

(b) *Test M*

This is the advanced form of Raven's 20-minute Progressive Matrices Test, consisting of 38 items, as used by the British War Office.

(c) *Test H*

This test was constructed by the Aptitude Test Section of the S.A.A.F. It consists of 62 items involving the solution of simple arithmetical problems. Thirty minutes were allowed for completion.

(d) *Test G*

This is a form of the Gottschaldt Figures Test. It was adapted by the Aptitude Test Section of the S.A.A.F. from the United States Army Air Forces' Test AC 121. It contains 45 items and 20 minutes are allowed for completion.

There is no point at this stage in embarking on a controversial academic discussion as to what these tests measure. For our present purpose it is sufficient to state simply that 'a test measures what it measures', and our problem is to find out whether this has any validity for the prediction of the criterion of success in the occupational field under consideration.

It was considered, however, that the results of these four tests should give a fairly adequate picture of the candidate's innate mental ability. Raw scores on the above tests were computed by simply summing the number of correct items.

To be complete this battery should have included a test of verbal ability. Unfortunately, the N.I.P.R. research work had not yet progressed sufficiently for a test to be included which would have been equivalent for both language groups.

(3) *Assessment of Performance in a 'Face-to-Face' Interpersonal Situation*
(*see Annexure E*)

A test situation was devised by the N.I.P.R., in which the candidate was required to interview and report on a female applicant for the post of personal assistant to a senior official. The candidate is supplied with the applicant's written application, testimonials and a statement of the job requirements. He is given a reasonable period in which to study these, then calls the applicant in for interview and finally submits his recommendations in writing. The role of the applicant is undertaken by an experienced female member of the N.I.P.R. staff, whose task it is (i) to assess and report on the candidate's handling of the interview, and (ii) to assess his personality make-up as revealed in this interpersonal situation. This test was designed to gain information on two major points, viz.—

(1) the candidate's over-all performance in an interpersonal working situation, and

(2) his insight and shrewdness in evaluating human material.

The situation was so designed that only candidates with a good measure of insight would detect the deficiencies in the applicant's personality and occupational record.

This test resulted in two separate assessments for each candidate:

(i) The interviewee rated each candidate in terms of the following items:

Self-confidence.

Presence.

Pleasantness of manner.

Ease of establishing social contact.

Ability to impose his personality on interviewee.

Perseverance at getting at facts.

Effective use of questions.

Effective use of data supplied.

Effectiveness of control of situation.

Appreciation of requirements of situation.

For this purpose a 5-point scale was used for each item where:

0=very inferior

1=inferior

2=low average

3=high average

4=superior

5=very superior

In addition the interviewee was requested to make an overall assessment of the suitability of the candidate as a trainee as judged from this test situation in terms of a 9-point scale:

A+ = exceptional
A = superior
A− = very good
B+ = high average
B = average
B− = low average
C+ = below average
C = poor
C− = very poor

Interviewees were instructed that a rating of B+ would indicate that they had judged the candidate to be 'just acceptable' as a trainee, and a B rating would indicate that he had 'just failed to make the grade'.

(ii) The candidate's report on the interview was later rated independently by three members of the N.I.P.R.'s technical staff.

For this purpose a 9-point scale was used similar to the one above.

These ratings were made in terms of the degree to which the candidate obtained and made a correct evaluation of the facts (both overt and covert) of the interviewee's case, and the business-like and convincing manner in which this evaluation was presented.

(4) *Assessment of Performance in Group-Test Situations*

These tests were designed to assess:

(i) The candidate's executive and administrative ability.

(ii) His potential leadership qualities.

(iii) His ability to cope with interpersonal relations in group situations.

(iv) Defects in personality make-up.

Two tests were used:

(1) The Leaderless Group Test.

(2) The Assigned Leadership Group Test.

Both tests approximate closely to situations with which senior administrative workers in any large concern would be faced in the course of their duties.

(a) *The Leaderless Group*

Each batch of candidates is formed into groups of eight, according to language medium, English and Afrikaans groups being tested separately. The group is seated round a table and given the following instructions:

We want you to imagine that you are delegates to a conference who have met for the first time to consider and give your recommendations on the following problem, viz.:

'Should South Africa accept, in industry, the principle of equal pay for equal work?'

[The subject for discussion was varied from time to time.]

During the discussion you can say what you like and conduct the proceedings in any manner you like, but, at the end, it is essential that you should, *as a group*, formulate definite recommendations on this question.

Although we (the assessors) shall be present during your discussion, we want you to ignore our presence as much as possible. We shall not interfere with your proceedings, nor take part in the discussion, and none of your remarks must be addressed to us.

You will be allowed one hour to complete your proceedings. Is everything clear? Are there any questions?

Right. Over to you!

A number of assessors are present during this test (in the present procedure, four representatives from the sponsor firm and two members of the N.I.P.R. staff). Their task is to report on and assess ten different aspects of each candidate's performance, viz.:

(1) Ability to express his ideas.

(2) Quality of contributions made.

(3) Attempted dominance over group.

(4) Deference received from group.

(5) Effective criticism of others.

(6) Ability to support own contentions and deal with criticisms of others.

(7) Amount of participation.

(8) Calmness and self-control (at ease).

(9) Pleasantness of manner.

(10) Ability to stick to the point.

The aim of the test is to place candidates in an ill-defined, unstructured situation, in which they are faced with a reasonably difficult problem. They have to think and act quickly, introduce order into the situation, formulate decisions and pilot them through the group, and compete with other candidates for leadership of the group. In such a situation the weaker candidates are edged out on to the fringe of the group, and the more capable and dominant members take over control. The situation enables assessors to gain insight into many aspects of the candidate's personality and to assess the leadership qualities of group members.

Each candidate was rated by each assessor in terms of the above items using a 5-point scale where:

0=very inferior

1=inferior

2=low average

3=high average

4=superior

5=very superior

3

In addition to rating the candidates on the items shown above, the assessors are required to write subjective reports on each candidate's performance and personality make-up as reflected in this situation.

(b) Assigned Leadership Group Test (see Annexure F)

It is necessary to supplement the information gained from the Leaderless Group Test by observing the candidates in a second group situation, where every possible chance is given for the display of abilities. The Assigned Leadership Test was designed to meet this need.

For this purpose a comprehensive memorandum was drawn up on a scheme for rehabilitating ex-servicemen by the establishment of a farming and quasi-industrial community centre. The memorandum contains a mass of relevant and irrelevant detail on this proposed centre. This project was in effect modelled on the same lines as the 'Island Story' used in the C.I.S.S.B. programme.

After the nature of the test has been outlined to them, each candidate is given a copy of the memorandum to study overnight and instructed to be ready on the following day to put before a committee his recommendations on certain aspects of the work involved in establishing such a community centre. *Twelve* topics relating to this task are listed, and each candidate is free to choose for detailed study whichever *three* topics appeal to him. On the following day the group of eight candidates assembles round a table and each candidate in turn is asked to take the chair and put his recommendations to the group on *one* of the topics he has chosen. He is allowed a total of 25 minutes in which to make his proposals and deal with the criticisms and suggestions of the other group members. Every candidate has a different topic to deal with and is given the same period of time in the chair.

The test situation makes the following demands on each candidate:

(1) Ability to grasp the essential features in a mass of detail.

(2) Ability to evaluate data and formulate a policy on one aspect of the establishment of the centre.

(3) Ability to marshal facts in support of his contentions.

(4) The ability to present his plan effectively and pilot his recommendations through the group.

(5) The ability to support his contentions, deal effectively with criticisms and suggestions, and the ability to weld the activities of the group into a meaningful whole.

(6) The ability to control the group effectively while in the chair.

(7) The ability to criticize constructively the policy of other candidates when they are in the chair.

(8) The personality make-up which enables him to cope with other people, gain their respect and lead them to a definite objective.

A number of assessors are again present during this test (four representatives from the sponsor firm and one member of the N.I.P.R. staff). The candidates are closely observed while in the chair and on the floor over a period of three hours, and assessments are made on the ten qualities previously listed in the Leaderless Group situation using the same rating scale. Finally after observing candidates in both the Leaderless and Assigned Leadership Tests, the assessors made an over-all assessment of the candidate's suitability as an administrative trainee on a 9-point scale similar to the one given above.

The raters were instructed that in making their assessment they should first of all decide whether they would or would not accept a candidate as a trainee on his performance in the two group-test situations. The standard of assessment was fully discussed by the assessors before the procedures commenced, and it was agreed that the minimum rating for acceptability as a trainee in terms of this scale was a B+. In other words, an assessor who rated a candidate as B+ was in effect saying 'In terms of the performance which I have observed in these two test situations, I regard this individual as "just acceptable" as administrative trainee'; a B rating would indicate that a candidate had just failed to make this grade. Scores above B+ would show the extent or degree of a candidate's acceptability and below B, the extent or degree of his rejection.

Apart from the more specific abilities which the group tests are designed to bring into play, these situations provide valuable observations on the candidate's behaviour, temperament and personality, and contributed greatly to the total clinical picture gained.

(5) *Written Project*

As administrative and executive ability is not only revealed in interpersonal situations, and, as it is known that certain people find the spoken word a difficult medium for self-expression, it was felt that candidates should be given an opportunity of showing what they could do 'on paper'. This would give those who could 'write like an angel but speak like poor poll' a chance of displaying their abilities unimpeded by personal factors. It is also considered that in many real-life situations, the 'gas-bags' get away with too much, and there is a tendency to overestimate a man's capabilities because of his capacity for self-salesmanship.

It was therefore considered necessary to assess the ability of candidates to deal with problem situations on paper. One written report was required in the Trial Interview Test. A second was devised in relation to the Sheltered Employment Scheme. Candidates were set the problem of studying the information given on the community centre, and drawing up a report on whether the centre could be made to pay its way at the end of three years.

This task involved the following problems:

(*a*) Weighing up all information available on the community centre project.

(*b*) An analysis of the capital and current expenditure available for running the scheme.

(*c*) The calculation of the deficit between current income and expenditure.

(*d*) The suggestion of practical ways in which this deficit could be made good.

(e) The use of relevant information to support these suggestions.

(f) The final decision on future prospects of the farm.

(g) The marshalling and presentation of these facts in a logical, concise and convincing manner.

There was no 'correct solution' to this written project, and more importance was attached to the method by which the candidate approached the problem and its solution, rather than the actual solution *per se*. Consequently assessors were instructed to rate in terms of

(i) the accuracy of the candidate's appreciation of the situation and the relevance of the factors which he had taken into consideration;

(ii) the convincing nature of his conclusions (either one way or the other), and the effectiveness with which he had marshalled his facts in support thereof.

Again the reports were marked independently by three members of the N.I.P.R. technical staff using the 9-point scale given above.

(6) *Relationships with Colleagues* (*see Annexure G*)

Throughout the test procedure assessors had opportunities to observe the candidate's ability to establish good relations with his colleagues, particularly in the trial interview, leaderless and assigned leadership groups and in the clinical interview. It was necessary in addition to discover how the candidates in any one group reacted to each other. They were in close contact for two days, in situations calling for both co-operation and competition. They were likely therefore to react to each other fairly strongly during this period. To measure these reactions candidates were asked at the end of the two-days test period to fill in a sociometric questionnaire, which measured their reactions to other members of the group. The main fields covered in this questionnaire were:

(a) Personal likes or dislikes for members of the group.

(b) Estimate of the ability of group members.

(c) Estimate of leadership ability of group members.

(d) Assessment of the nature of the relationship which each member established with the group.

(e) Choice of group members as possible work colleagues.

By use of this questionnaire, it was possible to gain a picture of how the group had reacted to each member of it, and so provide valuable information to supplement the impressions which the assessors had gained of the relationships within the group.

(7) *Personality Projection Tests*

The broad aim of projection tests is to present to the candidate a vaguely defined situation which he can deal with or interpret as he wishes. His reaction is likely to be an expression of his own personality, more particularly his aspirations, fantasies, emotional needs and tensions, which are projected into the material presented to him.

(*a*) *Self-description*

Each candidate is given $7\frac{1}{2}$ minutes in which to write a description of himself as a good friend would see him. When he has completed this he is asked to write a description of himself as an enemy or hostile critic would see him, and again given $7\frac{1}{2}$ minutes in which to complete the description. The limited time allowed in each case has the purpose of forcing the candidate to write quickly and spontaneously.

(*b*) *Incomplete sentences**

Each candidate is presented with three roneoed sheets containing 40 incomplete sentences, preceded by the instructions: 'Complete these sentences to express your real feelings. Try to do every one. Be sure to make a complete sentence.' Examples of a few sentences are:

    (i)   I like ....

    (ii)   My greatest fear ....

    (iii)   What worries me ....

    (iv)   Secretly ....

Again a limited time (20 minutes) is allowed to complete these sentences, in order to force the candidate to write as spontaneously as possible.

The main purpose of these two projection tests was to provide preliminary 'pointers' for the clinical interview. In each test the candidate gives information on himself which is useful to the interviewer. Many of the candidate's answers have a significance which he himself does not appreciate, and indicate areas in which his adjustment may be faulty or his personality unstable. By studying the candidate's responses on these two tests, the interviewer is able to draw up a list of points on which he can probe the candidate more deeply during the clinical interview.

(8) *The Clinical Interview*

The clinical interview is the focal point of the whole selection procedure, and is conducted only by the most experienced members of the N.I.P.R. staff. It takes place towards the end of the two-days testing period, by which time the interviewer has observed the candidate in many different situations. The interviewer makes as thorough a study as time will allow of all the information on the candidate that has been assembled during the various test situations. He notes gaps and discrepancies in the information presented, and in particular attempts to assess in which directions the candidate shows actual or potential weaknesses or deficiencies. He pays particular attention to information on the candidate's family background, in view of the importance of this factor in explaining the candidate's present personality. From all this information, the interviewer is able to prepare a rough plan of approach which he will use in the interview situation. It must be emphasized at this point that the aim of the clinical interview is not to catch the candidate out, but rather to make sure that no aspect of his personality which may influence his success as an administrator is left out of account.

---

* This test is an adaptation of the one developed by Rotter and Willerman (1947). See also Symonds (1947).

The interview is conducted as informally as possible, and the interviewer attempts to put the candidate at his ease so that he will speak as freely as possible, the good interview being more a friendly discussion than a cross-examination. Ideally, at least one hour is required with each candidate in this situation, but this is not always possible. At the end of the interview, the interviewer draws up a report on the candidate and gives an assessment of the candidate's suitability on the following five-point scale:

1. Reject.
2. Possible.
3. Probable.
4. Very likely.
5. Accept.

All tests mentioned in this chapter, including those reproduced in the Annexures, were made available to candidates in both English and Afrikaans.

CHAPTER IV

APPLICATION OF THE TEST BATTERY

IN ALL, A TOTAL of 536 applications were received. Of these 175 were employees of the Corporation and 361 were 'external' applications. Seven internal applicants either resigned from employment in the Corporation or withdrew their applications before the testing programme commenced, leaving a total of 168.

The composition of external candidates was as follows:

East Rand and Southern Transvaal	131
Pretoria and Northern Transvaal	77
Natal	37
Cape and Orange Free State	126
	371
Withdrawn applications	10
Total considered for screening	361

The final total of effective applicants was thus 529.

In accordance with the request of management all internal applicants were put through the test procedures, but in the case of external applicants a pre-selection was made on the basis of the written application received. Factors taken into consideration were:

(*a*) Academic or professional qualifications.

(*b*) Previous experience or employment history.

(*c*) Age.

(*d*) Active service during World War II.

(*e*) Special circumstances arising in any particular case.

All applications were studied independently by a committee of three consisting of two representatives of the Corporation and the N.I.P.R. Research Officer in charge of the project. Each candidate was given a rating on a seven-point scale $(-3, -2, -1, 0, +1, +2, +3)$ by each assessor according to degree of suitability. These independent ratings were later compared in committee and a final rating given to each candidate. These final ratings were not averages of the three ratings. Where there was disagreement among the assessors, the application was reconsidered and discussed until a final rating could be agreed upon. A statistical analysis of original independent ratings is interesting in that it revealed:

(1) A high degree of agreement between the ratings of the three assessors.

(2) Mean ratings of almost equal value for the three assessors, indicating that the standard set by each was virtually the same.

The actual results are as follows:

Table 6

Intercorrelations between Assessors (external applicants)			
	Assessor A	*Assessor B*	*N.I.P.R.*
Assessor A	—	·77	·79
Assessor B	—	—	·76
N.I.P.R.	—	—	—

Table 7

	Mean Ratings of Assessors (external applicants)		
	Assessor A	*Assessor B*	*N.I.P.R.*
Mean ..	—0·2247	—0·1199	—0·3371
Standard deviation	1·5440	1·4606	1·6002

As the result of screening, 233 applicants were invited to Johannesburg to attend the full selection procedures; of these 14 withdrew leaving 219 to be tested.

These candidates were formed into groups of eight. Two factors governed the formation of these groups : (a) the date on which the candidate was available for testing, and (b) the language medium. English- and Afrikaans-speaking candidates were formed into separate groups as far as possible to facilitate testing procedure. Within the limitation of these two factors each group was a random sample of the applicant population. The testing of candidates was carried out at the N.I.P.R. laboratory in Johannesburg from 16 November to 16 December 1948, and from 17 February to 4 March 1949, the testing time for each candidate being two days. It was possible, therefore, to deal with two groups of eight candidates during the two working days.

Before testing began, candidates were addressed by a senior representative of the Corporation and the N.I.P.R. Research Officer. The object of these addresses was to make sure that all candidates were fully acquainted with the implications of the whole method and programme of selection from both the Corporation's and N.I.P.R.'s points of view.

It was also made clear to all candidates that they could do the tests in whichever of the two official languages they preferred. The choice lay with the candidate, so that no candidate was handicapped by the language medium used.

The hours of testing were 8.30 a.m. to 12.30 p.m. in the morning, and from 2 to 5.30 p.m. in the afternoon. Arrangements were made for lunch, and tea was provided during the morning and afternoon intervals. Candidates were kept fairly busy during the two-days testing period, but had sufficient free time to prevent the development of undue fatigue. A copy of the testing time-table is given in Annexure A.

Every attempt was made to give each candidate a fair and equal chance to produce his best performance. During the clinical interview at the end of the procedure, each candidate was asked whether he had been given a fair chance to show his ability, and was given the opportunity to mention any circumstances which might have handicapped his performance. One candidate complained of a bad cold, but the rest, without exception, were satisfied that they had had as good an opportunity as the next man of proving their ability.

CHAPTER V

VALIDATION STUDY

BEFORE PROCEEDING TO a technical consideration of the validity of the present techniques, it is appropriate that certain existing deficiencies should be remembered. These may be listed as follows:

(a) THOSE ARTIFICIALLY IMPOSED

These were chiefly due to the decision, at short notice, by Management that all internal applicants should go through the procedures. Though expedient from the point of view of internal policy, this decision imposed severe strains on the testing programme by increasing considerably the number of candidates to be tested. The repercussions in terms of time and availability of experienced staff have already been referred to in an earlier section of this study. It is sufficient to mention here that the main disadvantage was the fact that the clinical interview—the key and focal point in the whole procedure—had to be curtailed after a certain date owing to shortage of trained staff. The result was that interviews had to be rushed to cover all candidates, and inadequate time was available to record systematic write-ups while the data were still fresh in the interviewer's mind. Though introducing a deficiency in certain respects, the decision to test all internal applicants was not without its advantages in others, viz. it provided a larger group of individuals on whom a follow-up study could be made. Nevertheless much valuable data have been lost or rendered useless for analysis, owing to the enforced departure from the strict system of controls which should discipline all research work.

(b) THOSE INHERENT IN THE PRESENT PROCEDURES

(i) One of the chief shortcomings of the present procedures was the relatively short time during which candidates were available for testing. Until this can be altered, if at all, the programme must be fitted into a period of two working days. This inevitably reduces the number of test situations that can be applied.

(ii) In their ideal form the procedures demand a three-day residential testing programme, where candidates gather at a 'guest-house' and live and work together with the assessors the whole time. This not only allows more time for tests, but also enables the assessors to get a more intimate knowledge of each candidate. Time and the lack of suitable accommodation precluded these arrangements in this case. Whether this is possible or desirable in the future or not, the more restricted programme must inevitably suffer from these limitations.

(iii) Owing to the particular arrangements demanded by certain essential procedures, and the difficulty of fitting these into the normal working hours of two days, it was not possible to allow the clinical interviewers sufficient time to scrutinize all data on each candidate before interviews. This time is essential for preparing the strategy of each interview which has to be different in each case, and is the *sine qua non* for success in these situations.

(iv) For the same reasons it was not possible to allow the assessors in the group-test situations to meet *after each session* and discuss their findings on each candidate before proceeding further. The task of the assessors is an extremely difficult one, calling for a high degree of skill in a very complicated, highly structured, and often fast-moving situation. The assessment of the candidate's make-up during the interaction of personalities calls for sustained concentration, quick observation, and the ability to look below the surface. Consequently the margin of error may be great, and this can only be reduced by a comparison of findings among the assessors, where each one is called upon to substantiate his conclusions, and is reminded of incidents which he missed. The final assessment of candidates should be reached in this way, and not by the crude arithmetical average of assessor ratings. Furthermore, as a result of these discussions there often emerge important gaps in a candidate's make-up which the assessors want checked. These can be passed on to the clinical interviewer for special investigation. Refinements of this type were impossible in the present programme.

Despite these defects of which the N.I.P.R. was aware at the time, there remained sufficient confidence in the essential features of the testing programme to enable the Institute to proceed with reasonable assurance of success. This confidence was moreover enhanced by the knowledge that the usual method of selection, depending upon a letter of application plus testimonials and a board interview had been proved in the past to be unsatisfactory. Both the letter of application and the testimonials give only that information which the applicant wants to impart. Furthermore, the formal interview usually does not enable the selecting authority to elucidate the additional information required, nor will it reveal anything but the most obvious defects in a candidate. Considerable skill is required to read between the lines of a letter of application, to notice the significance of omissions in the presentation of facts, and finally, to obtain the relevant information from candidates, which will fill in the gaps. Even the most skilled observers have been unable to make decisions on the evidence from these three sources alone. This fact was proved during the war.

(1) The reliability of tests used

Some psychological authorities still consider the determination of test-reliability to be an important requirement of test-validation. This is presumably because of the belief that the higher the reliability of a test, the greater its validity.

In the light of Loevinger's (1947) recent contribution to this subject, in which she examines critically the theories of earlier authorities, and in view of McNemar's (1949) carefully studied admonitions on the derivation and use of the formulae concerned, one must agree that the concept of reliability as at present defined and used is highly unsatisfactory.

We have, in a previous publication (Arbous, 1951) given our reasons for the rejection of the customary definition of reliability as having little physical significance in the present context, and indicated an alternative line of approach which we have attempted to adhere to in this work as far as circumstances would permit.

However, in order to avert the criticism that the arguments previously stated constitute a convenient philosophy in the present instance, we shall report the estimates of the 'reliability' of the tests used in this research project, but, in doing so, shall follow Goodenough's (1936) advice:

> What we should do, I think, is to relegate the use of the term 'reliability' to the limbo of outworn concepts, and express our results in terms of the actual procedure used.

(a) Pencil-and-Paper Tests

The reliability of pencil-and-paper tests A(F), M, H, G had been established by previous research before being used in this testing programme. The odd *v.* even-item correlations in this project are quoted as follows for the sake of interest.

The results are:

Table 8

Test	No. of Items	Odd *v*. Even-Item Coefficient of Correlation		No. of Cases*
		Uncorrected for Length	Corrected by Spearman-Brown Formula	
A(F)	65	·81	·90	306
M	38	·83	·91	306
H	62	·84	·91	257
G	45	·82	·90	257

There is little point here in entering into a theoretical discussion as to whether the basic assumptions could be guaranteed in this instance. In all probability the above figures are an over-estimate but they would seem to indicate that the tests were reliable for the group on which they were used.

(b) The Remaining Test Situations

The above technique could not be applied in the case of those test situations where assessments or ratings were made by various judges or testers. However, care was taken at the outset to arrange these procedures in such a way that some control would be exercised over this factor, and some indication of the reliability of these tests would be obtained. This was done in the following manner. It was arranged that at least three independent assessments were made of each candidate in every situation where this was practicable. It was thus possible to calculate the consistency with which candidates were marked in terms of a *correlation coefficient of agreement* between the ratings of each pair of assessors. If there were unsatisfactory agreement the ratings on that particular test-situation were rejected altogether. In the case of the two group tests, the final rating

* These numbers include the 219 cases tested plus some subsequent groups.

score of each candidate was arrived at by combining the ratings of assessors between whom a high degree of agreement was found to exist.

The Spearman-Brown formula enables us to estimate the reliability of the combined ratings of two assessors in terms of ρ_{xy}. Sichel (1950 a) has given a more general formula of which the Spearman-Brown is a particular case, and which enables us to estimate the minimum reliability of the combined ratings of three or more assessors.

The results of this study will then be reflected in terms of the coefficients of agreement between assessors, and (for what it is worth in terms of the assumptions which are necessary), the estimate of the 'reliability' of combined scores will be given in terms of Sichel's formula. This procedure will be adopted in the case of all test-situations and in the case of the criterion itself.

(i) *Trial interview test*

The candidates' reports on this interview were rated independently by three members of the N.I.P.R. staff. The coefficients of agreement were as follows:

Table 9

	A	B	C
Assessor A Assessor B Assessor C		·22	·59 ·14

These coefficients were far too low to be of any value. This test was therefore rejected. Further research will have to be done to improve the standard of assessment here.

By the very nature of the test it was impossible to have more than one interviewee's report on the candidate. The reliability of these reports could not, therefore, be assessed by this means. However, a straightforward frequency distribution of ratings yielded the following results:

Table 10

Rating	Tally Strokes	Frequencies
A+	11	2
A	11111. 11111. 11	12
A−	11111. 11111. 11111. 1111	19
B+	11111. 11111. 11111. 11111. 11111. 11	27
B	11111. 11111. 11111. 11111. 11111. 11111. 11111. 11111. 11111.	45
B−	11111. 11111. 11111. 11111. 11	22
C+	11111. 11111. 11111. 11111. 11111. 11111.	30
C	11111. 11111. 11111. 11111. 11111. 11111. 11111. 11111. 11111.	45
C−	11111. 11111. 11111. 11	17
		219

The bi-modality of this distribution, after careful analysis, clearly indicated that the ratings were suspect, and that the test should be rejected.*

(ii) *Written project on the sheltered employment study*

The coefficients of agreement between three independent N.I.P.R. assessors were as follows:

Table 11

	A	B	C
Assessor A		·67	·66
Assessor B			·66
Assessor C			

Here agreement is satisfactory. The test was regarded as reliable and retained for the validation study. The candidate's final score was computed by simply adding the ratings of the three assessors. Applying Sichel's (1950 a) formula, the reliability of the combined rating obtained in this way is estimated to be at least 0·86.

(iii) *Final rating on the two group test situations*

The assessors in these situations consisted of a member of the N.I.P.R. staff, together with four representatives of the Corporation. The resulting coefficients of agreement between the final ratings of these judges were as follows:

Table 12

	N.I.P.R. Staff member	A	B	C	D
N.I.P.R. Staff member .		·77	·77	·66	·56
Assessor A			·85	·71	·62
Assessor B				·70	·63
Assessor C					·68
Assessor D					

The agreement here is satisfactory with the exception perhaps of that between Assessor D and the rest. As it was not likely that so many assessors would be available in future, it was decided to take the ratings of the three assessors among whom there was closest agreement. These were N.I.P.R. staff member, Assessors A and B.

Again the candidates' final scores on this test were computed by simply summing the ratings of the N.I.P.R. staff member, Assessors A and B. Applying Sichel's (1950 a) formula the reliability of the combined rating obtained this way is estimated to be at least 0·93.†

* A detailed study of this phenomenon has been made by A. L. Pons (1951).

† A complete study of these group tests has been made in a separate publication, Arbous, A. G., and Maree, J. (1951). The analysis of results shows excessive halo between the combined ratings of assessors on each test situation and the final rating. This justifies the use of the assessor's final rating only in this validation study.

(iv) *The clinical interview*

It was impossible to arrange for all candidates to be clinically interviewed by more than one psychologist. The reliability of assessments in this situation could, therefore, not be estimated.

In conclusion scores on the following tests were considered to be sufficiently reliable to be included in the validation study which follows:

(*a*) Test A(F).

(*b*) Test M.

(*c*) Test H.

(*d*) Test G.

(*e*) Written Project.

(*f*) Two Group-Test Situations.

(2) THE VALIDITY OF TESTS USED

Under ideal circumstances the total applicant population should be tested first, and the whole group should then proceed to the training scheme and later to the field of employment in question. From a follow-up study at various stages one would ascertain which had turned out to be failures and which successes. The validity of the test predictions could then be measured against these latter results. Obviously this procedure was completely impracticable in the given circumstances, and one had to be content with follow-up studies of a different nature.

However, the technical point to be considered here is that even if this procedure were carried out there would still remain the problem of finding a measure of success which could be expressed in some quantitative form. The matter is somewhat simplified when one is dealing with a specific training programme which is terminated by some qualifying examination (e.g. trade test or university examination) where 'success' is reflected in terms of examination marks. Yet even this measure is not adequate, for the standard of marking may vary from centre to centre, or year to year, and in any case these marks only indicate 'success' at the beginning of a man's career.

The failure-rate when actually on the job has still to be considered. We thus see that the criterion itself can still be wrong in predicting 'actual success' achieved later.

These difficulties can be summarized under the following headings:

(i) that of obtaining a criterion of 'success' in some quantitative form;

(ii) having done so, that of making sure that the criterion itself is reliable just as any test is;

(iii) that of ensuring that the criterion used is a good indication of ultimate 'success' on the job.

These considerations have led to a vast amount of theoretical speculation concerning the nature of 'success'. More recently Davies (1950), Stott (1950) and Reeves (1950) have discussed the philosophical and practical aspects of the problem by way of a literary symposium in *Occupational Psychology*. It is not our intention to enter this controversy by attempting to cast further light on the absolute meaning of the term. The arguments of these authors should however be heeded, for they encourage the investigator to be extremely cautious in regard to his claims for the predicting efficiency of any test battery, and force him to define quite specifically just what is being predicted, and what the words 'success' and 'failure' mean in terms of the criterion used.

The investigator is not usually allowed much choice in his selection of a criterion. Consequently, whether or not he has solved the riddle as to what is the 'universal yardstick of success', he is more often than not compelled to make do with follow-up data of a limited type and from a limited number of sources. The procedure then of validating his test battery against criteria of this nature is quite justifiable provided he defines quite specifically what it is predicting, and limits his claims of efficiency strictly to the terms of his definition.

The remaining portions of this chapter will, therefore, be concerned with a consideration of the type of criteria used in the present investigation, the validity of the tests in predicting those that might be regarded as reliable, and finally, an evaluation as to what the adopted criterion signifies and the advantage in the battery's capacity to predict it.

(a) The First Study with Criteria 1, 2, and 3

In the first follow-up study three independent criteria were used.

(i) Criterion 1 (C_1)

This was determined as follows:

$$C_1 = \frac{(\text{Present salary}) - (\text{Starting salary})}{\text{Length of service in years}}$$

Only employees with two or more years service were considered.

The above formula naturally reflects the rate of financial advancement per year of employment. Such a criterion could not be considered in a situation where annual increments were granted on an automatic basis provided the incumbent had not been guilty of gross dereliction of duty. The investigators were given to understand, however, that such was not the case in the Corporation where the general policy was to start employees off on a fairly low notch and to grant subsequent increments in such a way that present salary was considered to be commensurate with performance on the job—if need be, more than one increment being given in a year. Furthermore, it was quite usual for *double increments* to be given in the case of outstanding service. It will be appreciated from the above considerations that, had this employment policy worked as was intended, the rate of financial advancement in the Corporation's service should have been a fairly good indication of the potential level of ability of the individual.

There are obviously many defects in the use of this criterion as a measure of potential ability in administrative work, e.g. often, to correct one anomaly in salary, several collateral adjustments have to be made which at times are based on more spurious considerations. Space does not permit of a lengthy examination of these deficiencies which must be

obvious. The investigators felt that as the problem of obtaining any satisfactory criterion was difficult, no possibility should be overlooked.

(ii) *Criterion* 2 (C_2)

A system of job-grading had recently been introduced in the Corporation where every administrative and clerical post was classified into one
of the following grades with its appropriate salary scale and rate of
increment.

Table 13

Grade	Salary Scale
U.G.—ungraded	1,080
Grade A . .	$900 \times 60 - 1,080$
B . .	$750 \times 50 -$ 900
C . .	$600 \times 30 -$
	$660 \times 40 -$ 750
D . .	$480 \times 30 -$ 600
E . .	$390 \times 30 -$ 480
F . .	$300 \times 30 -$ 390
G . .	$120 \times 30 -$ 300

The rationale behind the use of these grades as a criterion is principally
that an individual's appointment or promotion to a job is usually an indication of the value which the employing organization places upon his
capacity, and the higher up the scale the individual is at the moment, the
better are his chances of success in the administrative field. Here again
the criterion suffers from many patent inadequacies which are principally
associated with the defects of job evaluation techniques and employee
assessment—to say nothing of the influence of the factors of age and
experience which are necessarily associated with potential ability.

(iii) *Criterion* 3 (C_3)

This criterion consisted of a straight rating of potential success in
administrative work on the basis of past record. A senior official in the
staff office was requested to scrutinize the personal files of the candidates
and, on the basis of supervisors' reports, comments and the withholding or
granting of increments, to make an efficiency rating on a four-point scale.
This rating of past efficiency was intended to provide an indication of
future success. This was not entirely a subjective affair, for the assessor
was clearly briefed as to the importance to be attached to the number of
special increments given or increments withheld during an employee's
occupational history. The inadequacies of this criterion are chiefly those
associated with the reliability of an efficiency rating system, and supervisor's reports on employees.

Having collected the necessary data for these three criteria on approximately 100 existing employees, a reliability test was carried out by cor-
relating the candidate's potential ability as assessed by the one criterion
with that as determined by the other two. The results are as follows:

Table 14

Coefficients of Correlation between Criteria			
	C_1	C_2	C_3
C_1		·24 ($n = 92$)	·34 ($n = 92$)
C_2			·42 ($n = 111$)
C_3			

Although the relationships between C_3 and the other two are significant the degree of relationship is nowhere high enough (i.e. above 0·7 at least) to enable one to say that any two of the criteria are satisfactory measures of the same thing. It is still possible for one to be valid, assuming that the other two are not, but one could not demonstrate this except by subjective argument, which will not do for our purpose. A further and perhaps more cogent reason for the rejection of these criteria was the fact that they applied only to internal employees, only two of whom had actually been selected as trainees, and the investigators could see no way of including the remaining fourteen selected candidates in these studies. For the same reason no attempt was made to estimate the agreement between these three criteria and those which follow.

In examining further criteria particular attention was paid to the fact that these had to allow for the inclusion of the existing selected trainees. Clearly a good deal of time would have to lapse before any follow-up material on these candidates could be considered worth while. It was decided that a period of *one year* should be regarded as the essential minimum for this purpose.

(b) *The Second Study with Criteria 4, 5, and 6*

(i) *Criterion 4* (C_4) *(see Annexure B)*

This criterion consisted of a rating scale so constructed as to enable a supervisor to rate each trainee in respect of a number of defined abilities and attributes. Detailed instructions and item definitions were supplied with the scales in order to ensure uniformity of interpretation as far as possible. Care was taken to ensure that an employee was only rated by an assessor who had known him for some considerable time and was well acquainted with his work. Supervisors were in fact asked whether they felt really confident of their ability to pass judgement on the candidates in question, and requested to strike off the list all those about whom they were in doubt. The one disadvantage of this method was, however, that by the very nature of employment it was not possible to have all candidates rated by all the assessors. This meant in fact that each employee was rated by only one supervisor, and it was consequently not possible to test the latter's ratings for consistency and uniformity of standard. This simply meant that one could not have the bread buttered on both sides, and where it was a question of choosing between 'thorough acquaintance before rating' on the one hand, and 'testing for reliability' on the other, the investigators decided on the former as the more desirable alternative— particularly as some indication of reliability would be yielded later by comparison of these results with those obtained from the other criteria.

When completing each rating scale assessors were requested to leave blank all items where they genuinely felt they lacked sufficient evidence for solid judgement. It was considered that nothing was to be gained by mixing shrewd observations with guesses, and as an additional safeguard assessors were reminded that any rating, unsupported by some factual statement, would also be excluded.

A final point must be mentioned in regard to this rating scale. Assessors were asked to base their judgement on actual observations. The ratings of candidates thus constituted assessments of actual or present ability rather than of potential ability for the future. It is important to note this difference between C_4 and the other criteria which follow.

The sixteen selected trainees were included in this study by requesting all supervisors under whom a portion of their training period was spent to complete a rating scale in respect of each. As these trainees were moved about fairly frequently during the year, it was possible to obtain at least five independent assessments on each of them. Thus the inadequacies of short acquaintances were somewhat compensated for by multiple assessments in the case of these individuals. The final ratings thus consisted of the average of several assessments.

As was only to be expected, not all items on the rating scale were used by the assessors. It was, therefore, only possible to utilize those items which had been consistently used throughout. This naturally meant a reduction in the final items used, and also in the number of cases constituting our total sample. The numbers dropped from 132 to 97: a loss of approximately 26% of our data, which could be quite serious.

The following items were retained for calculating the final score:

General mental ability . .	Intelligence
	Reasoning ability
Special abilities	Bilingual ability
	Language ability
	Number ability
	Social ability
Personality qualifications .	Drive
	Self-confidence
	Dependability
	Personal maturity
	Motivation

A detailed analysis of the ratings on these items was carried out and it was found best under the circumstances to calculate the final score on C_4, by simply adding together the individual ratings on items.

(ii) *Criterion 5* (C_5) (*see Annexure C*)

After all candidates had been rated on C_4 and the scales had been handed in by the assessors, the latter were requested to *grade* each candidate (in respect of whom they had previously completed a rating scale) on a nine-point scale in accordance with what they considered to be his occupational ceiling, i.e. the highest position to which he was likely to advance in the future given all the opportunities and encouragement for doing so. Thus—

Table 15

A+	A	A=	B+	B	B—	C+	C	C—
Senior Adminis- trator	Adminis- trator	Junior Adminis- trator	Senior Execu- tive	Execu- tive	Junior Execu- tive	Senior Clerical	Clerical	Junior Clerical

Again detailed instructions and definitions were supplied to each assessor to ensure uniformity of concept. The existing sixteen selected trainees were incorporated in this study in a manner similar to that described above—several gradings being obtained for each trainee and the mean being taken as his final grading.

Assessors were specifically instructed to judge the candidates purely in terms of potential ability for the future.

Gradings of this type were completed in respect of 132 cases.

(iii) *Criterion* 6 (C_6) (*see Annexure D*)

Again after all gradings had been completed and handed in, the same assessors were requested to co-operate in respect of the same individuals, in order to furnish material for a third criterion. A novel technique was applied here, having two distinct advantages which are not immediately apparent. Briefly, assessors were given the list of candidates whom they had stated they knew and felt competent to judge. They were asked to assume that *no other* candidates were available and *some* had to be selected from the list in question. The instructions then proceeded as follows:

> We would like you to indicate which candidate you consider to possess the *most potentiality*, and *least potentiality*, for training and development in the field of administrative work, by carrying out the following procedures.
>
> (a) From the list of candidates supplied select the *one* whom you consider to be the *best suited*. Remove his name from the list and record it opposite No. 1 below.
>
> From those names that are left on the list again select the *best suited*, remove his name from the list and record it opposite No. 2.
>
> In the case of your particular list we should like you to repeat this procedure (x) times.
> (1)
> (2)
> (3)
> (4)
> etc.

(b) From the names that are left on the list after procedure (a) has been carried out we ask you to select the *least suited*; remove his name from the list and record it opposite No. 1.

Again in this particular case we should like you to repeat this procedure (x) times.

(1)
(2)
(3)
(4)
etc.

The first advantage of this technique was that by choosing x (i.e. the number of repetitions required for each list) in the appropriate manner, the procedure resulted in the individuals on the list being grouped in three broad categories:

(i) high

(ii) average

(iii) low

in the proportions 1 : 2 : 1 , which are the expected proportions for normal distribution in terms of a single variable. This has important advantages for statistical analysis of data.

Thus if one assessor had twenty names on his list and was requested to repeat his selections *five* times in each case, these individuals would, as a result, be divided into—

5 high

10 average

5 low.

In this way a degree of comparability was ensured between the selections of different assessors with different names on their lists.

A candidate's 'final score' on this criterion merely consisted of one of the three broad ratings mentioned above.

The second major advantage of this procedure was the fact that the technique involved was something with which assessors were more familiar —it was a more meaningful 'game' to them, the rules of which they were in a better position to understand, having, one supposes, adhered to them on many previous occasions. The task before them was not new and they were not distracted by definitions of terms and relative degrees. They merely had to survey the list before them and pick the best or reject the worst on successive occasions, and moreover this procedure was not repeated *ad absurdum*. Admittedly, the end result was merely that the total group of candidates was ultimately divided in three classes, but it was felt that this broad differentiation would provide another yardstick for estimating the reliability of C_4 and C_5, by an independent means which lent itself admirably to statistical techniques.

This procedure could only be applied where the number of individuals on the assessor's list was large enough to warrant this broad grouping. Consequently the number of cases in this study dropped from 132 to 123, which was not as serious a loss as in the case of C_4.

Of far more concern to the investigators was the problem of including the sixteen selected trainees in this study. This was finally managed as follows.

As mentioned above, each assessor divided his list of candidates into three broad categories: high, average, and low. We then returned to each assessor with this grouping of his candidates together with the list of selected trainees. The assessor was then requested to compare each trainee in turn with the candidates on his list, and to place the trainees one by one in one of the three categories which he considered appropriate by comparison with the individuals already in it. Assessors only rated those trainees whom they had had under them for some period of training. The result was that several such ratings were obtained from different assessors for each trainee. The results are given in Table 16 below, and reflect also the final rating for each trainee which was computed by statistical means from the raw data provided. (See Appendix, section 1 (a).) It will be noticed that the assessors did not all give the trainees high (H) ratings, and that there are many averages (A's) and in two cases lows (L's). This indicates that the assessors were fairly independent in their judgements and not unduly influenced by the fact that the individuals were selected trainees. Furthermore two trainees end up with only (A) assessments.

It will be remembered, also, that the 'selection' procedure involved in this criterion allowed individuals to be rated as 'high' who had not been selected as trainees.

Table 16

Trainee	Assessors									n	Mean Rating	Final Class
	1	2	3	4	5	6	7	8	9			
1 . .	A	H	H	—	H	A	—	H	H	7	0·953	H
2 . .	H	H	A	—	H	—	—	—	H	5	1·069	H
3 . .	—	H	H	—	H	H	—	H	H	6	1·339	H
4 . .	H	H	H	—	H	H	H	—	H	7	1·339	H
5 . .	—	—	—	—	H	—	—	—	H	2	1·339	H
6 . .	H	H	H	H	H	H	H	—	H	8	1·339	H
7 . .	A	A	H	H	A	A	H	—	A	8	0·494	A
8 . .	A	L	A	H	L	—	—	A	A	7	−0·206	A
9 . .	H	H	H	—	H	—	H	—	H	6	1·339	H
10 . .	A	—	H	—	H	—	H	—	A	5	0·799	H
11 . .	A	A	H	H	H	A	H	H	H	9	0·889	H
12 . .	H	—	H	—	H	H	—	—	H	5	1·339	H
13 . .	H	H	H	H	—	—	—	H	H	6	1·339	H
14 . .	—	A	H	—	—	A	—	H	H	5	0·779	H
15 . .	—	H	H	H	—	H	—	—	H	5	1·339	H

Table 17

Class Intervals for Final Class	
− ∞ to − ·7961	Low
− ·7961 to + ·7655	Average
+ ·7655 to + ∞	High

Having collected all the data necessary for criteria 4, 5, and 6, it is now possible to see to what extent these are consistent measures of the same 'thing' which we hope represents 'success' in the administrative field of work. The same estimate of reliability was made in the case of these criteria as was made in the first study with criteria 1, 2 and 3, and in the case of assessor ratings on the group tests, viz. by the calculation of a coefficient of agreement or consistency between the respective pairs.

Table 18

	Coefficients of Inter-Correlation		
	C_4	C_5	C_6
C_4		·315 $n = 97$	·268 $n = 97$
C_5			·718 $n = 123$
C_6			

These results indicate that between C_5 and C_6 there is a degree of consistency which is satisfactory for our purposes. It will be remembered that the rating scale used in C_4 provided an assessment of the individual's present capacity whereas the other two emphasized rather the candidate's potentiality for development. The agreement between C_5 and C_6 enables us to use these measures as a means of validating our test procedures, since the test scores were *unknown* to the various assessors passing judgement. In this case, applying Sichel's (1950 *a*) formula the reliability of the combined criterion is estimated to be at least 0·84. The technique for combining assessments on C_5 with those on C_6 is given in Appendix, section 2.

This then is the most 'reliable' yardstick against which we can measure the predicting efficiency of our tests, and our next concern will be to find some numerical estimate of this efficiency in the case of each test used.

(3) CORRELATION BETWEEN TESTS AND CRITERIA, AND THE CONSTITUTION OF THE FINAL TEST BATTERY

From the above it will be seen that there are three criteria against which the tests can be validated, viz. C_5, C_6, and C_{5+6}.

The validity coefficients in respect of those tests which have been accepted as 'reliable' are given in Table 19 below:

Table 19

Test	Validity Coefficients					
	C_5 $(n=132)$		C_6 $(n=123)$		$C_{5+6}(n=123)$	
	r	SE_r	r	SE_r	r	SE_r
A (F)	·48	·07	·54	·06	·53	·06
M	·40	·07	·35	·08	·43	·07
H	·34	·08	·36	·08	·33	·08
G	·28	·08	·29	·08	·28	·08
Written Project (W.P.) .	·54	·06	·46	·07	·53	·06
Final Rating on 2 Group Tests (F.R.) . . .	·55	·06	·46	·07	·60	·06

In all cases the r's are greater than three times the standard errors of estimate, indicating that the validity coefficients are significant above the

1% level. Regression weights and multiple correlations are next calculated to determine:

(a) which criterion shall be used in our present study;

(b) which tests constitute the most efficient battery for the prediction of the criterion chosen.

For these calculations the intercorrelations between the tests themselves are required. This raises a more serious question. C_5 assessments are available for 132 cases, but C_6, and hence C_{5+6} assessments, were only made in respect of 123. On the other hand, test scores are available for 219 individuals. Should then the intercorrelations between tests be carried out in respect of $n = 219$, 132, or 123 cases?

In order to dispose of this difficulty it is necessary to make a comparison of the three groups with respect to their means and standard deviations in order to determine whether there is any statistically significant difference between them.*

The results are given in Tables 20 and 21 in respect of all tests used:

Table 20

Tests	Comparison between Means of Test Scores for different n's					
	Means (on arbitrary scale)			Critical Ratios $t = \dfrac{d}{SE}$		
	219	132	123	$\dfrac{n = 219}{n = 132}$	$\dfrac{n = 219}{n = 123}$	$\dfrac{n = 132}{n = 123}$
A (F). .	0·105	0·098	0·138	0·063	0·293	0·899
M . .	0·402	0·508	0·480	1·056	0·714	0·648
H. . .	0·183	0·114	0·187	0·690	0·040	1·639
G. . .	−1·525	−1·508	−1·488	0·104	0·203	0·264
W.P. . .	−4·484	−4·636	−4·504	0·707	0·086	0·462
F.R. . .	−5·589	−6·091	−5·935	2·038	1·293	1·468

Table 21

Tests	Comparison between Standard Deviations of Test Scores for different n's					
	Standard Deviations (on arbitrary scale)			Critical Ratios $t = \dfrac{d}{SE}$		
	219	132	123	$\dfrac{n = 219}{n = 132}$	$\dfrac{n = 219}{n = 123}$	$\dfrac{n = 132}{n = 123}$
A (F). .	1·871	1·870	1·875	0·325	0·198	0·258
M . .	1·822	1·824	1·823	0·426	0·277	0·284
H. . .	1·796	1·894	1·867	1·026	0·656	0·695
G. . .	3·064	3·175	3·476	0·878	0·738	0·173
W.P. . .	3·910	3·790	3·841	0·272	0·191	1·127
F.R. . .	4·471	4·523	4·586	2·677	1·959	1·338

* The usual formula for the significance of difference between m's and S's cannot be used in this case because $n = 123$ is contained in $n = 132$ and both are contained in $n = 219$. The formulae used in the present instance are given by Skellam (1949). (See Appendix, section 3.)

Only in one instance is the value of the critical ratio larger than 2·5. We are therefore not justified in rejecting the hypothesis that there is no difference between the various groups with regard to the two statistical moments compared. It would seem reasonable to assume therefore that the three groups are representative of each other with respect to their scores on all tests used in this study and that the intercorrelations between tests based on either $n = 219$, 132, or 123 could justifiably be used in our estimation of the multiple correlation coefficient of the test battery. In the present instance we shall use the intercorrelations based on the sample of 132 as being perhaps more appropriate, in that this group is more representative of that in which criterion assessments were obtained than is the group of 219.

The results are given in Table 22.

Table 22

| Tests | Inter-correlations between Tests $n = 132$ | | | | | | | Validity Coefficients | | |
	A(F)	(M)	H	G	WP	FR	CI	C_{5+6} $n=123$	C_5 $n=132$	C_6 $n=123$
A (F)		·67	·56	·58	·42	·48	·55	·53	·48	·54
M			·37	·52	·28	·36	·41	·43	·40	·35
H				·32	·35	·28	·25	·33	·34	·36
G					·24	·35	·33	·28	·28	·29
Written Project (W.P.) . . .						·43	·40	·53	·54	·46
Final Assessment in Group Tests (F.R.)							·66	·60	·55	·46
Clinical Interview (C.I.). . . .								·54	·52	·45
Criterion (C_{5+6}) .										

These results show that there is a good deal of overlap between tests A(F), M, H, and G. Of these A(F) has the highest validity coefficient and should therefore be retained. Test M is also retained in the pivotal condensation as having the next highest validity coefficient.

The only other serious overlap is between the final assessment in two group tests (F.R.) and the clinical interview. In view of this overlap, in addition to the inability to estimate the 'reliability' of the clinical interview, it is considered that ratings from this test situation should not be included in the final battery score, although the interview itself should not be eliminated from the testing programme. Thus where the final assessment in group tests will allow personality qualities to have their influence in final prediction, the data from the clinical interview will usually supply a more detailed diagnosis of personality make-up.

Intercorrelations and validity coefficients in respect of the following tests are finally submitted to analysis by pivotal condensation in order to determine the relative weights of the tests and the predicting efficiency of the final selection battery, with respect to each of the criteria.

1. Test A (F).

2. Test M.

3. Written Project.

4. Final Assessment on two Group Tests.

The results of this analysis are given in Table 23.

Table 23

Criterion	Test Weights in Multiple Regression Equation (Variables in S-units)				Multiple Correlation Coefficients		
	A (F)	M	W.P.	F.R.	R_e	SE	R_o
C_5	·187	·059	·300	·254	·649	·050	·645
C_6	·384	—	·234	·118	·608	·057	·579
C_{5+6}	·225	·064	·239	·309	·677	·049	·668

The estimate of the multiple correlation coefficient is given by R_e. To test the applicability of this mathematical model the weights are then ploughed back into the original data, the battery raw scores are normalized graphically, and the observed correlation coefficient between these and the criterion calculated for C_5, C_6, and C_{5+6} (R_o) .*

We have now assembled sufficient information to enable us to answer the question as to which criterion to use in the present study.

From this we can conclude:

(a) *In terms of R's*

While the R_e's for all criteria are satisfactory, and the agreement between the observed and expected is good in each case, that from C_{5+6} is the highest.

(b) *In terms of Regression Lines*

Rectilinearity of regression is not as satisfactorily demonstrated in the case of C_5 as it is in the other two. The regression of battery scores on this criterion may in fact be curvilinear. The correlation surface to be dealt with in this case is not as satisfactory for our subsequent purposes as are those from the other two criteria.

(c) *In terms of Test Weights*

C_5 gives most weight to W.P. and F.R. Both these procedures are as yet unstandardized, and may well vary in time. They both involve subjective ratings by assessors. The possibility of these tests going out of control statistically is therefore great, and consequently one cannot place much confidence in the consistency of the test battery's predicting efficiency where so little weight is given to only one standardized pencil-and-paper test.

In the case of C_6 the reverse is the case: too much weight is perhaps given to the written tests (A(F) and W.P.), and too little to F.R. which analysis has shown to be most likely a measure of 'personality' qualities.†
We consider, therefore, that these attributes would have too little influ-

---

* The method for calculating the correlation coefficient in the case of C_6 and C_{5+6} is given in Appendix, section 1(b).
† *vide* Arbous, A. G., and Maree, J. (1951) for conclusions in this regard.

ence on predicting efficiency for an occupation where they are known to be of great importance.

In the case of C_{5+6} there is a more favourable balance between the influences which the pencil-and-paper and personality tests have on the final battery score. The largest weight is received by the latter, but more is given to A(F) than in the case of C_5 which, as a counter to unstandardized procedures, would help to maintain the consistency of prediction on subsequent occasions.

Because of the above considerations we conclude that:

(a) the best criterion to use in the present circumstances is C_{5+6};

(b) the most efficient test battery for the selection of administrative trainees which has so far been established consists of

(i) Test A(F);

(ii) Test M;

(iii) The Written Project (W.P.);

(iv) Final Rating on two Group Tests (F.R.);

(v) The Clinical Interview—for explanatory purposes only;

(c) this battery's efficiency in predicting this criterion (C_{5+6}) is represented by a final validity coefficient of 0·68;

(d) no other tests used in this project in their present form will improve this efficiency. If this is to be achieved further research is needed (i) to improve the existing tests and (ii) to discover new ones which will make their own unique contributions to the efficiency of the battery.

(e) It must also be borne in mind that the 'reliability' of the criterion itself is far from perfect. We shall not in this study tinker with our observed validity coefficient by estimating what it would have been had the criterion been 100% reliable, for the reason that we can give no assurance that our estimate of the 'reliability' of C_{5+6}, in terms of the coefficient of agreement, is valid, and we can see no way of guaranteeing that the underlying assumptions on which the formulae are based have not been violated.

We shall therefore in this study work with what may be a conservative estimate of R, namely 0·68.

It would be possible in subsequent chapters to proceed with the analysis along parallel lines for C_5, C_6, and C_{5+6}. It is considered, however, that not much would be gained by this procedure, over and above that which has been summarized for comparative purposes in an appropriate section of the Appendix, section 4. Furthermore, such a procedure would tend to confuse the essential features of a picture which will be difficult enough to sketch in any case.

(4) THE PHYSICAL SIGNIFICANCE OF THE CRITERION

It is stated here quite specifically that the test battery, as validated, is only predicting the opinion of supervisor-assessors as to the success which the individual is likely to make of administrative work in the future. This is based on observed performance over a period of at *least* one year.

No claim is made that this judgement represents *actual success* in this field in terms of any universal yardstick.

Consequently 'success' in this study is defined in terms of the criterion as a *high* rating by supervisors, and no attempt will be made to add any further meaning to this statement.

The physical significance of a final validity coefficient of $R = 0.68$ can, therefore, be stated as follows:

> This coefficient of correlation merely indicates the overall efficiency of the test battery in predicting, on the basis of two days' testing procedures, what the opinion of supervisors on the job will be, after at least one year's acquaintance, of the potential capacity which the individual has for administrative work in the present Corporation.

The value of this might well be questioned. It might be asked, for example: 'If the opinion of supervisors is to be accepted, then why not use C_{5+6} as a basis for selection in the first place and dispense with the elaborate procedures?' The answer is given in terms of the fact that the judgement of supervisors is based on at least one year's observation on the job, and battery scores on only two days' procedures. The test battery can therefore make the claim that in this time it can predict to the efficiency of $R = 0.68$ what the opinion of supervisors will be after one year.

Naturally in these terms the test battery could not add much to the Corporation's knowledge of existing employees with one year's service, for in this case management would merely have to consult its supervisors for an opinion in terms of the C_{5+6} rating scales. It is therefore more particularly in regard to new employees that the battery will make its contribution to management. In this regard, it will be able, with an efficiency of $R = 0.68$, to predict what the supervisors will think of a man after one year's personal observation. The gain here can be quite considerable from many points of view, particularly if one considers the cost of training which is expensive, the serious implications of mis-selection in senior posts in terms of disrupted industrial relations, depreciation of morale, incompetence, etc. There is no need here to elaborate these considerations, provided only that one does not lose sight of them.

Regarding the philosophical question as to the extent to which the supervisor's opinion may be regarded as an indication of a *universal criterion of success*, we would add that we are not convinced that this is such a serious consideration as it might appear at first sight. Is it not the person who wears the shoe who can tell whether it pinches? If the system of values of management is at variance with the universal yardstick of success does it help the organization to select people who, in terms of the universal standard are 'successes' but who, in terms of the system of values obtaining in the organization, are not? The short-term objective of selection procedures is merely the following:

Unless there is good reason to suppose that the organization's system of values is anti-social, it is justifiable to standardize a system of selection which will produce, with a known degree of consistency and validity, personnel who will measure up to that system of values.

CHAPTER VI

THE OPERATING CHARACTERISTICS OF THE FINAL TEST BATTERY

BEFORE PROCEEDING TO an appreciation of the full significance of a validity coefficient of $R = 0.68$ for the present test battery the data should be submitted to further statistical treatment.

In the first place it is necessary to calculate in terms of the multiple regression equation for C_{6+5}, each candidate's battery raw score in standard scores for the whole sample of 219 cases.

These scores should then be normalized graphically (see Appendix, section 5) to yield final battery standard scores. As a result we have in terms of the normalization of the 219 cases these scores for the 123 cases in whom we are interested in our validation study against the criterion. The results of this process for both the 219 and 123 samples are given as follows in respect of means, standard deviations and χ^2 tests for goodness of fit with a theoretically expected normal frequency distribution.

Table 24

	m	S
$n = 219$	49·98860	9·92265
$n = 123$	49·49185	9·97180

Table 25

B.S. Scores Class Intervals	$n = 219$			$n = 123$		
	f_o	f_e	$\dfrac{(f_o - f_e)^2}{f_e}$	f_o	f_e	$\dfrac{(f_o - f_e)^2}{f_e}$
75 — 80	1 ⎫	}0·4 ⎫		1 ⎫	}0·3 ⎫	
70 — 75	4 ⎬ 13	1·1 / 3·6 ⎬ 14·7	0·196	4 ⎬ 10	0·6 / 2·0 ⎬ 8·3	0·348
65 — 70	8 ⎭	9·6 ⎭		5 ⎭	5·4 ⎭	
60 — 65	22	20·1	0·180	8	11·3	0·964
55 — 60	34	32·8	0·044	14	18·4	1·052
50 — 55	42	41·9	0·0002	24	23·5	0·011
45 — 50	40	41·9	0·086	27	23·5	0·521
40 — 45	33	32·8	0·001	18	18·4	0·009
35 — 40	18	20·1	0·219	11	11·3	0·080
30 — 35	13 ⎫	9·6 ⎫		11 ⎫	5·4 ⎫	
25 — 30	3 ⎬ 17	3·6 ⎬ 14·7	0·306	⎬ 11	2·0 ⎬ 8·3	0·878
20 — 25	1 ⎭	1·1 / }0·4 ⎭		⎭	0·6 / }0·3 ⎭	
	219	219·0	1·086 χ^2	123	123·0	3·863 χ^2
	P [5, 1·086] = 0·954			P [5, 3·863] = 0·572		

From these results we see that, though the normalization was carried out *only* on the basis of 219 cases, where one expects the mean standard score to be 50, and the standard deviation to be 10, and the frequency distribution to be normal in terms of the P value from the observed χ^2, the same characteristics may be said to hold for the 123 individuals taken from this group. The distribution of their battery standard scores is also normal and again we have evidence that the group we are studying is representative of the total group of 219 cases.

We then proceed to plot these 123 battery standard scores in the form of a bivariate frequency distribution against C_{5+6} (the distribution of the latter having been normalized by scaling in terms of the proportions of the sample falling within the three categories, and representing the mid-points of these classes in terms of S-units). (See Appendix, section 2.)

The result is given in Fig. 1. The observed correlation coefficient is $R_o = 0.67$ where, in terms of the mathematical model it is expected to be $R_e = 0.68$. The agreement between theory and observation is thus satisfactory, and one is justified in working with a coefficient of 0.68 in future calculations. The regression lines were found to be rectilinear, thus indicating that we are in all probability dealing with a fairly normal bivariate frequency distribution. It has been our object so far to establish this as far as possible by the process of normalization in order that the properties of the normal bivariate surface for correlation may be applied with reasonable accuracy to our observed data.

It should, in passing, be mentioned that the normalization of the univariate marginal distributions does not automatically ensure this desirable result.

This preliminary study is of a crucial nature for the subsequent analysis which follows, for the reason that the mathematical models which are evolved are inapplicable to our data unless these conditions can be satisfied.

We have so far already indicated that in all probability the conditions are satisfied, which justifies our proceeding. Later on, additional evidence will be produced which will confirm that in fact the mathematical models are a satisfactory representation of the observed data in this research project. *Thus in all subsequent graphs which illustrate the theoretically predicted results of selection we have plotted the observed probabilities or proportions (whichever the case may be) based on the actual data to hand. The agreement between the theoretical curves and observed points will be seen to be satisfactory.*

We can now proceed to an examination of the full significance of the final validity coefficient of $R = 0.68$.

In any selection procedure, whether by aptitude test battery or any other means, the selector can commit two fundamental errors, viz.—

(a) that of selecting candidates who will prove to be failures;

(b) that of rejecting candidates who would have been successes.

Unless the selection procedures are perfect the above two errors will always occur in varying proportions depending upon the efficiency of the techniques used.

There are, moreover, two parties concerned in these errors, viz. the selector and the applicant himself.

CRITERION (C_{5+6}) ASSESSMENT

β

	Failure		Success	
	Scale in Standard Measures			
Class Intervals	Low $-\infty$ to $-\cdot300$ $-\cdot9982$	Average $-\cdot300$ to $+\cdot643$ $+\cdot1594$	High $+\cdot643$ to $+\infty$ $+1\cdot2467$	f
75 - 80			1	1
70 - 75			4	4
65 - 70			5	5
60 - 65	1	4	3	8
55 - 60	1	6	7	14
50 - 55	8	10	6	24
45 - 50	11	13	3	27
40 - 45	10	6	2	18
35 - 40	6	4	1	11
30 - 35	10	1		11
25 - 30				
	47	44	32	123

Battery Standard Scores

Correlation Coefficient r = ·67

BIVARIATE DISTRIBUTION SHOWING
FREQUENCY WITH WHICH BATTERY
SCORES ARE ASSOCIATED WITH
CRITERION ASSESSMENTS

FIG. 1

Sichel (1950 *b*), by applying standard mathematical formulae associated with the normal bivariate surface, has developed two functions which he has called 'Operating Characteristics'.

These are closely associated with the real interests of the above two parties, and describe the risks involved in a selection procedure carried out by means of an aptitude test battery.

These he has defined as follows:—

(*a*) '*The Selector's Operating Characteristic* gives the probability of the applicant's success in the job as a function of his battery performance.' (i.e. his final battery score.)

(*b*) '*The Applicant's Operating Characteristic* gives the probability of the applicant's selection as a function of his true ability and/or personality.' (i.e. his criterion score.)

The predicting efficiency of any test battery was stated earlier to depend on the magnitude of the validity coefficient (0·68) between battery scores and the criterion of success (C_{5+6}). In order to calculate this coefficient it was necessary to draw up a bivariate distribution or scatter diagram, showing the frequency with which scores on the test battery were associated with the final ratings on the criterion (see Fig. 1).

In this diagram the line dividing success and failure on the job has been drawn between the average and high assessments in the criterion. This decision was made in terms of the original assignment which was to select candidates of outstanding ability. This means that individuals rated as *high* were regarded as having been judged 'potential successes' by the Corporation's assessors. Thus in all, 32 of the 123 candidates were considered to fall in this category.

(1) THE SELECTOR'S OPERATING CHARACTERISTIC

Using the appropriate formula (Appendix, section 6) we calculated the theoretical probabilities of success for the whole range of test battery scores, by means of which the equation was graphed in Fig. 2. This shows that, theoretically, with a battery standard score of 66·5 a candidate's probability of success (as measured by the criterion) is 0·75, i.e. out of 100 candidates *with this score* seventy-five would be expected to succeed. Furthermore, if one does not want to run a risk greater than 0·25 that any individual selected will prove a failure (i.e. a probability of at least 0·75 that he will be a success) he must, according to Fig. 3, place the battery pass-mark or cut-off point at 66·5 standard score (S.S.). Such an assurance of success, however, can only be achieved at the expense of rejecting 94·5% of the total applicant population. Under certain circumstances this may be desirable. It is important to remember in fixing the cut-off point, that gains in one direction are only achieved at the expense of losses in another. The profit and loss account of selection in terms of this operating characteristic will be more fully considered later.

In passing it should be noticed that the observed probabilities of success based on Fig. 2 were plotted by means of crosses, against the midpoints of the class-intervals. The agreement between theory (solid curve) and

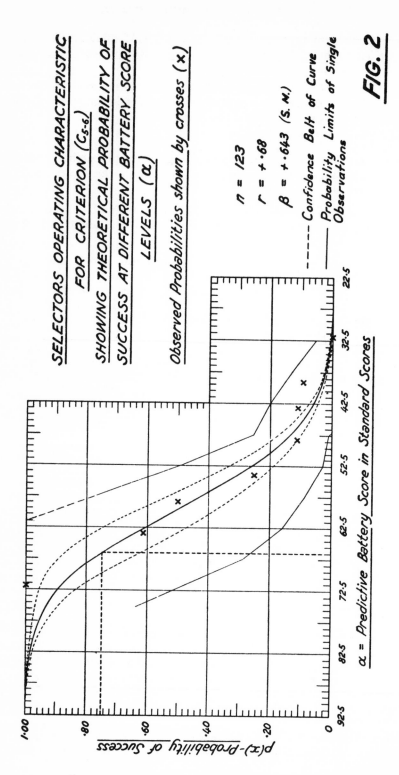

SELECTORS OPERATING CHARACTERISTIC
FOR CRITERION (C_{S-6})

SHOWING THEORETICAL PROBABILITY OF
SUCCESS AT DIFFERENT BATTERY SCORE
LEVELS (α)

Observed Probabilities shown by crosses (x)

$n = 123$

$r = +.68$

$\beta = +.643$ (S.M.)

- - - - Confidence Belt of Curve

———— Probability Limits of Single
        Observations

FIG. 2

α = Predictive Battery Score in Standard Scores

p(x)-Probability of Success

5

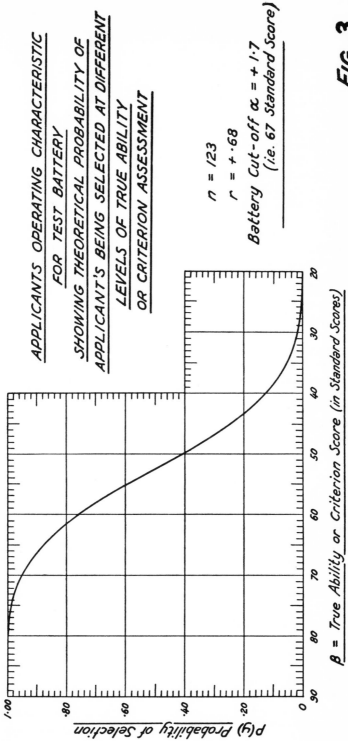

APPLICANTS OPERATING CHARACTERISTIC
FOR TEST BATTERY
SHOWING THEORETICAL PROBABILITY OF
APPLICANT'S BEING SELECTED AT DIFFERENT
LEVELS OF TRUE ABILITY
OR CRITERION ASSESSMENT

n = 123
r = +·68
Battery Cut-off α = +1·7
(i.e. 67 Standard Score)

FIG. 3

β = True Ability or Criterion Score (in Standard Scores)

P(y) Probability of Selection

observation (crosses) is satisfactory, indicating that our assumption of normality of the distribution is not seriously in error.*

(2) THE APPLICANT'S OPERATING CHARACTERISTIC

The candidate's operating characteristic indicates how good a man's chances are of being selected by means of the testing procedure for the standard currently set. To illustrate this it was decided to set the qualifying standard in such a way that no man recommended by the N.I.P.R. would have less than a 76% chance of being found satisfactory as an administrative trainee. Fig. 2 shows that the minimum acceptable final battery score would be 67 S.S. Again using the appropriate formula (Appendix, section 6) the probabilities of selection at any true ability level can be calculated. In Fig. 3 these probabilities are presented graphically for a battery selection score of 67 S.S.

A study of this graph will reveal immediately that a candidate with outstanding true ability is almost certain to be selected, whereas the poor candidate has almost no hope if selection is done in terms of this aptitude test battery. Both conditions are in the interest of the candidate as well as management, since in the former case the individual is spared the repercussions of future disillusionment and frustration. In short, with conventional selection procedures the chances of a candidate with *high* ability are not necessarily much greater than those of a man with *low* ability, whereas with test selection they increase steadily with increase in real ability. Testing therefore fulfils a vital service to the applicant as well as to management, and those who object to selection in terms of validated tests are really objecting to fair play and the service of their own interests.

Observed probabilities could not be plotted about the theoretical curve in Fig. 3, as the number of classes in the criterion were too few.

Having explained the principles of selecting efficiency of the test battery as far as the selector and applicant are concerned, it now remains to illustrate how management's interests are served by means of this technique.

(3) MANAGEMENT'S OPERATING CHARACTERISTICS

The employer's interests are not necessarily identical with those of the selector. The latter is concerned with the candidate's probability of success at different battery score levels—the former, in this particular case, is more concerned with

(i) what proportion of candidates selected at and above a given battery score level will eventually turn out to be successful?—i.e. if thirty people are selected at and above battery score level *x*, how many of these will prove successful administrators?†

(ii) is the gain in the percentage of selectees who are successful so great an advance over other selection techniques that the cost

---

* The probability belt of the curve, and the probability limits |of single observations were plotted by means of Sichel's formulae (1952).
† This idea is developed from the work of Taylor, H. C., and Russel, J. T. (1939).

of the more elaborate test procedures is a paying and economic proposition?

To answer these questions we need some definition of what is meant by the efficiency of test battery selection. It is clear that some formulation of this can only be given by comparing test battery selection with the more conventional selection technique with regard to the gain in the percentage of selectees who are successful. Sichel (1950 b) has pointed out that 'Not much is known about the effectiveness of non-test selection programmes. It will certainly vary from employer to employer depending entirely on the shrewdness, insight and knowledge of the selector engaged in the task of appointing personnel. Most likely the efficiency will lie somewhere between blind chance and test selections. However, in order to establish the usefulness of a battery, we must have a standard against which to measure the efficacy of aptitude tests. For this reason the varying and unknown efficiencies of conventional procedures are of no avail. It is therefore proposed to use pure chance selection as a standard.'

The efficiency index of our test battery is consequently defined as:

$$(H_1) = \begin{bmatrix} P_1 \\ \text{battery selection} \\ \text{where } r = 0.68 \end{bmatrix} - \begin{bmatrix} P_1 \\ \text{selection by technique} \\ \text{where } r = 0 \end{bmatrix}$$

where P_1 in both cases $= \dfrac{(\text{No. of successes selected}) \times 100}{\text{Total no. of selectees}}$

Here (H_1) represents the gain in the percentage of selectees who are successful when selection is undertaken by a test battery which correlates $r = 0.68$ with the criterion, over the corresponding percentage when the technique used has a zero correlation $(r = 0)$ with the criterion.

Conversely in terms of selection errors or failures, the efficiency index may just as conveniently be given as:—

$$(H_1) = \begin{bmatrix} \pi_1 \\ \text{selection by technique} \\ \text{where } r = 0 \end{bmatrix} - \begin{bmatrix} \pi_1 \\ \text{battery selection} \\ \text{where } r = 0.68 \end{bmatrix}$$

where π_1 in both cases $= \dfrac{(\text{No. of failures selected}) \times 100}{\text{Total no. of selectees}}$

Here (H_1) represents the corresponding reduction in the percentage of selectees who are failures when selection is undertaken by the test battery over the corresponding percentage when the other technique is used.

Because of the complementary relationship:

$$P_1 = 100 - \pi_1$$
$$\text{and} \quad \pi_1 = 100 - P_1,$$

the actual value of (H_1) will be the same when calculated by either method, and in further considerations we shall confine ourselves to the use of P_1 which is the more positive objective of selection. Thus for all *practical* purposes (H_1) represents nothing more than the test battery's gain over chance selection in increasing the percentage of successes in the selected group. It is emphasized, however, that the cut-off score (a), (i.e. the qualifying mark on the test battery), and the dividing line between success and failure (β) in the criterion (i.e. between those judged to have high and average potentiality for administrative work), must be kept as constant values for both battery selection and the other technique when the values of P_1 or π_1 are being calculated.

This definition of efficiency will change under different circumstances as will be seen later, and will only apply where management is purely concerned with the proportions of successes which exist in the selected group.

The method for establishing the values of P_1 for a given test procedure, and for a given cut-off score, is best illustrated by reference, again, to the normal bivariate surface upon which correlation is based.

Fig. 4 represents, in the case of a particular sample, the usual type of bivariate frequency distribution which is used to calculate the product-moment coefficient of correlation (r). The numbers in the cells represent the frequencies with which scores on the test battery (y-axis) are associated with scores on the criterion scale (x-axis). The cut-off score 'a' is represented by the vertical plane AB, and the division between success and failure on the criterion (β) by the vertical plane CD. If the bivariate distribution is normal, and if we imagine the class-interval to be greatly reduced in size, thereby increasing their numbers considerably, and the 'n' of the sample to increase infinitely, then the distribution tends towards a smooth surface, 'somewhat resembling a policeman's helmet'. This is known as the normal bivariate surface, applicable to the total population of which the former group was a random sample. The horizontal cross-section of this figure can be conveniently represented by an ellipse, and Fig. 5 then becomes a shorthand representation of Fig. 4. The equation to this normal surface is known and the problem of calculating the various proportions in which we are interested becomes amenable to mathematical treatment by the use of standard tables.

It will be readily observed from Fig. 5 that:

   (i) ACB represents the proportion of the total population selected.

  (ii) ADB represents the proportion of the total population rejected.

 (iii) CAD represents the proportion of the total population failures.

 (iv) CBD represents the proportion of the total population successes.

Furthermore:

  (v) CEB represents the proportion of the total population who are selected and successful.

 (vi) AEC represents the proportion of the total population who are selected and failures.

(vii) BED represents the proportion of the total population who are rejected and successful.

(viii) AED represents the proportion of the total population who are rejected and failures.

Furthermore, the percentage of selectees who are successful is represented by:

$$P_1 = \frac{\text{CEB} \times 100}{\text{ACB}}$$

As it is reasonable to assume that our bivariate distribution is normal, all the above proportions can be calculated mathematically, provided

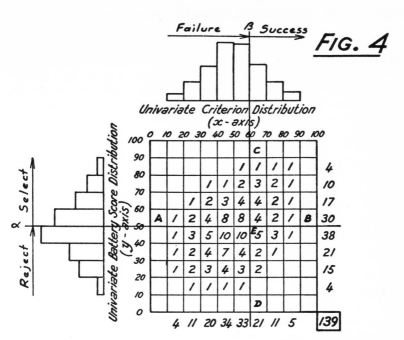

Univariate Criterion Distribution
(x - axis)

BIVARIATE FREQUENCY DISTRIBUTION
FOR CORRELATION

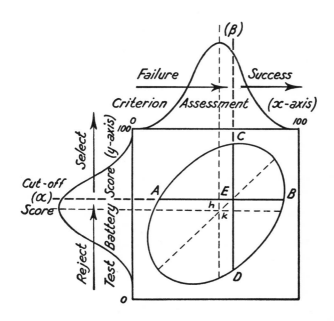

THE NORMAL BIVARIATE SURFACE

FIG. 5

the values of α and β and the correlation coefficient (r) are known. In our particular case α and β can be stated in terms of standard measures which indicate the proportion of the applicant population which falls above or below the two dividing marks. By reference to Pearson's Tables (54) Part II, pp. 78–137, and putting $\alpha = 1\cdot7 = h$, $\beta = 0\cdot643 = k$, the proportion CEB is derived for the given correlation coefficient $r = 0\cdot68$. Naturally the value of CEB will vary as the cut-off score α is raised or lowered, and in this way it is possible to determine the proportions for the whole range of possible cut-off scores in order to observe how the efficiency of the test battery varies, as the standard of acceptance is raised or lowered. Furthermore, once having ascertained the value CEB, the values of AEC, AED, DEB can all be determined by simple arithmetic; since for example AEC = ACB − CEB, and ACB is known to be the area of the normal curve lying above $\alpha = 1\cdot7$. These proportions can then be graphed, and this is in fact what the appropriate curves in Fig. 6 represent. For $\beta = 0\cdot643$ and $r = 0\cdot68$ the different proportions can now be read off at a glance for the different values of α.

Again it should be noted that the observed proportions based on Fig. 6 were plotted against the limits of the class-intervals, and satisfactory agreement is noted between the theoretical (continuous) curves, and the observed points (circlets and crosses).

Thus at $\alpha = 1\cdot7$ (a 67 standard score) we have the following represented here as percentages *of the total population.*

Table 26

	Percentage of Total Population		
	Failures	Successes	Total
Selected. . .	0·7%	3·8%	4·5%
Rejected . .	73·3%	22·2%	95·5%
Total . . .	74·0%	26·0%	100·0%

From the above table the percentage of selectees who are successful is calculated as follows:

$$P_1\text{[test battery where } r = \cdot68] = \frac{3\cdot8 \times 100}{4\cdot5} = 84\%$$

This then is the value of the first term in our equation for the efficiency index (H_1), when $\alpha = 1\cdot7$.

When our cut-off score is lowered to $\alpha = 0$ (i.e. a standard score of 50) marked changes occur in the respective proportions reflected in the above table. These would then become:

Table 27

	Percentage of Total Population		
	Failure	Success	Total
Selected. . .	27·7%	22·3%	50·0%
Rejected . .	46·2%	3·8%	50·0%
Total . . .	73·9%	26·1%	100·0%

At this cut-off score level of $a = 0$:

$$P_{1[\text{test battery where } r = \cdot 68]} = \frac{22 \cdot 3 \times 100}{50 \cdot 0} = 44 \cdot 6\%$$

It is an extremely salutary exercise to work out similar rough tables for different a values, for only in such a way can one appreciate just what the repercussions are when the line between select and reject is drawn at different levels. The set of graphs in Fig. 6 in fact enables management to appreciate at a moment's notice what the full consequences will be in the case of this particular test battery. The information is highly significant for the determination of selection policy.

These considerations will be discussed more fully later. Before doing so it is necessary to return to our estimate of the test battery's efficiency.

It now merely remains for us to estimate the corresponding proportions which would result from the application of some selection technique which had zero correlation ($r = 0$) with our criterion, and to deduce the appropriate value of P_1 in this case.

The corresponding series of graphs for

$$r = 0 \qquad \beta = 0 \cdot 643$$

are given in Fig. 7.

Again from these a similar table can be drawn up as before. This is given in Table 28, which also includes data from Table 26 for the purpose of comparison.

Table 28

	Percentage of Total Population					
	Selection by Battery where $r = 0 \cdot 68$ $a = 1 \cdot 7$ $\beta = 0 \cdot 643$			Selection by Technique where $r = 0$ $a = 1 \cdot 7$ $\beta = 0 \cdot 643$		
	Failure	Success	Total	Failure	Success	Total
Select. .	0·7	3·8	4·5	3·3	1·2	4·5
Reject .	73·3	22·2	95·5	70·7	24·8	95·5
Total . .	74·0	26·0	100·0	74·0	26·0	100·0
	$P_1 = 84 \cdot 4$			$P_1 = 26 \cdot 7$		

Thus, the efficiency index of the battery, at a cut-off score of 67 ($a = 1 \cdot 7$) is estimated to be

$$(H_1) = (84 \cdot 4 - 26 \cdot 7)\% = 57 \cdot 7\%$$

Tables similar to Table 28 above can be drawn up for each possible a value, and the percentage of selectees (P_1) who are successful can be worked out as above for each cut-off score in the case of both battery selection ($r = 0 \cdot 68$), and selection by a technique having zero correlation ($r = 0$). The respective percentages can then be graphed as in Fig. 8. In this case we have shown the curve for P_1 only: the corresponding values of π_1 can be simply deduced by subtraction ($100 - P_1$). The resulting efficiency index (H_1) can then be calculated as shown above for each cut-off score. These values of (H_1) can be graphed in a manner which will

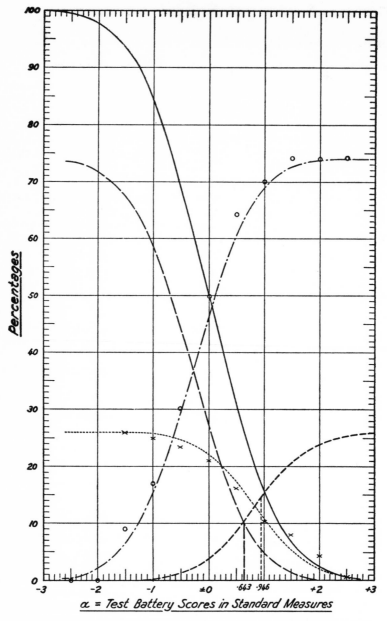

GRAPHS SHOWING PERCENTAGES OF TOTAL POPULATION

1. Who are selected ————————
2. „   „   „   and successes ·············
3. „   „   „   „   failures —— —— ——
4. „   „ rejected „ successes — — — — — —
5. „   „   „   „   failures —·—·—·—·—·—

At different values of Battery Cut-off Score (α)

r = +·68   β = +·643 (Standard Measures)
Observed percentages plotted by × and ○

FIG. 6

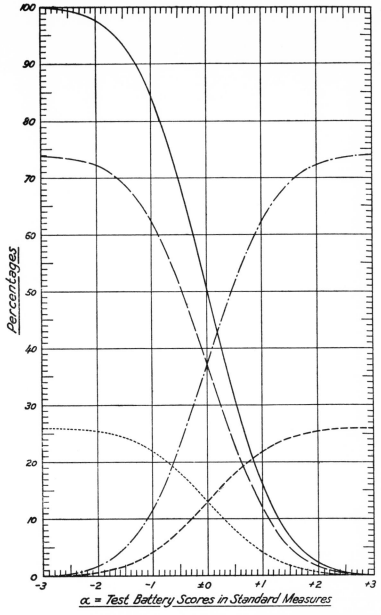

α = Test Battery Scores in Standard Measures

GRAPHS SHOWING PERCENTAGES OF TOTAL POPULATION

1. Who are selected ——————
2. „   „   „   and successes ·················
3. „   „   „   „ failures —— —— ——
4. „   „ rejected „ successes ── ── ── ──
5. „   „   „   „ failures ──·──·──·──

At different values of Battery Cut-off Score (α)

$r = 0$ $\beta = +\cdot 643$ (Standard Measures)   FIG. 7

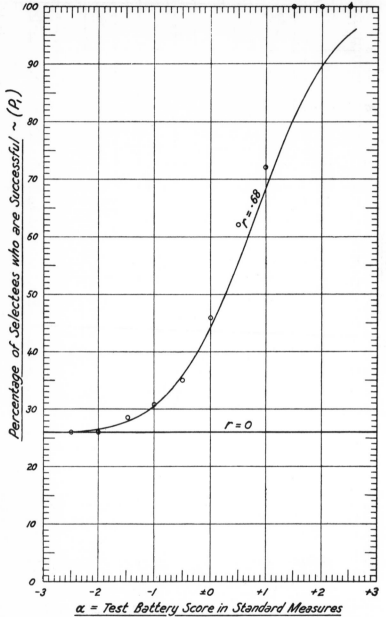

Percentage of Selectees who are Successful ~ (P₁)

α = Test Battery Score in Standard Measures

GRAPHS SHOWING PERCENTAGES OF SELECTEES (P₁)
WHO ARE SUCCESSFUL AT DIFFERENT
CUT-OFF SCORES (α) FOR

(a) Test Battery Selection, where r = ·68 } β = +·643
(b) Selection by Technique, " r = 0 } (Standard Measures)

Observed percentages plotted by ○

FIG. 8

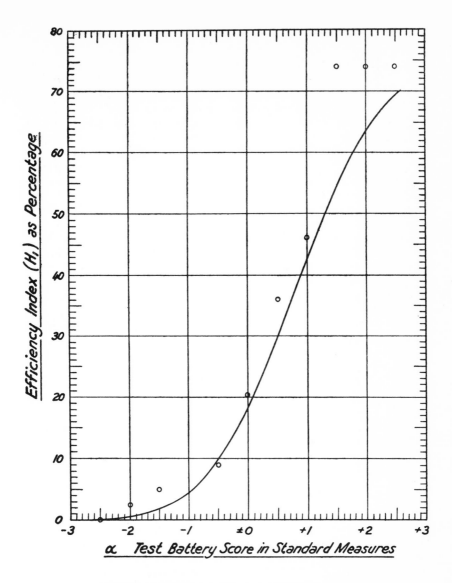

GRAPH SHOWING TEST BATTERY EFFICIENCY
INDEX (H₁) FOR DIFFERENT VALUES
OF CUT-OFF SCORE (α)

$r = \cdot 68$
$\beta = + \cdot 643$ (Standard Measures)
$n = 123$

Observed percentages plotted by ○   *FIG. 9*

indicate the efficiency of battery selection at the different cut-off levels. The appropriate graph is represented in Fig. 9, e.g. if the test battery cut-off score were set at 50 standard scores (i.e. $a=0$) the efficiency index of the battery would be 18·5%. This means that if 100 candidates were selected at this level by test battery, there would be 18·5 *more* successes, or 18·5 *less* failures in this selected group than would be the case if selection were undertaken by some procedure having zero correlation with the criterion. The gain at this level of cut-off is not very great. On the other hand the curve rises quite sharply, and the corresponding gain at a cut-off score of 65 (or $a=1·5$) would be 54·5%, i.e. there would be more than half as many more successes in the group selected by the test battery. The gain here is quite considerable especially when the serious consequences of mis-selection for important positions are taken into account. Naturally the *actual* number of people selected from the total group would be smaller at this level, as would the actual number of successes selected as the curves in Fig. 6 will indicate. In efficiency, however, we are concerned purely with the percentage of successes or failures in the selected group.

It is here recommended that the operative cut-off score for our test battery in the selection of administrative trainees should be placed at between 60 and 67 standard scores or ($a = +1$ or $+1·7$). Under these circumstances the efficiency of selection by means of this battery will be between 42% and 58%.

The operating characteristics and the selecting efficiency of the test battery have now been fully illustrated by the sets of graphs given in the preceding figures. A detailed study of these graphs will indicate what happens when selection is undertaken by means of this technique, and what the results are of fixing the battery cut-off score at various levels. It is important, when reaching a decision on this point, that all the graphs should be referred to in order to appreciate the full consequences of the decision—no single graph will give the whole story, and it will usually be found that advantages in one direction will be offset by disadvantages in another. In certain circumstances these disadvantages may not be serious, or may not matter at all. The graphs, however, will give a clear picture of all consequences in deciding on the cut-off point to be used. By this means management will be placed in full possession of the facts which should be carefully evaluated before reaching any decision: the selection policy can therefore be determined in advance with a full knowledge of the consequences. A further advantage to be considered is the fact that the selection procedures are standardized, and the above graphs will indicate the results *in the long run of events*. On the other hand, when using unstandardized techniques for selection, such as the usual board interview, one can never depend on the outcome. In certain instances, where the board is singularly astute or lucky, its efficiency in selection may well be greater than that of the test battery. There is, however, no guarantee that the high standard will be maintained. On subsequent occasions its efficiency may drop to zero because of changing circumstances or membership of the board. Under such conditions the determination of selection policy, or the planning of subsequent training procedures, or the provision of adequate numbers of competent staff to fill posts, becomes an extremely hazardous undertaking. With battery selection one can anticipate with a known degree of confidence just how policy will work out and future requirements be met. This consistency is in itself a considerable gain.

To illustrate the consequences of selecting at different values of a, Table 29 has been constructed.

It is of equal interest to illustrate what happens when the whole process is put into reverse. This is indeed what generally happens when management is deciding on a manning policy. The type of question to be answered in this instance is:

> Given (a) that it is desired to select 14 applicants, or (b) that 22 *successful* selectees will be needed in the future, where must the battery cut-off score be placed in order that the requisite number of candidates be forthcoming?

These questions can easily be answered once the number of total applicants is known. For example if there were 200 applicants, then it is seen from the table and the appropriate graphs that 6·9% or $\dfrac{13\cdot8}{200}$ of the applicant population are selected by placing the battery cut-off score at 65 S.S.; or, to answer question (b), that 11% or $\dfrac{22}{200}$ of the applicants are selected *and successful* at cut-off score 60. In this way, by reference to the appropriate graphs, management will know in advance where to place the cut-off score in such a way that its manning requirements will be met. It will, moreover, know at what approximate expense in training wastage (% selected and failures) these results will be achieved. Thus Fig. 8 indicates that at 65 S.S. the training wastage will be $(100-80\cdot6) = 19\cdot4\%$. At 50 S.S. it will be $(100-68\cdot8) = 31\cdot2\%$. In planning its training and manning policy management will be in a position to make allowance for these factors if desired, or decide just what training wastage can be tolerated, and how far its needs will be fulfilled in the future. By a careful scrutiny of these graphs management will be in a position to weigh in advance the pros and cons of its selection policy, in terms of training costs on the one hand, and the urgency of manning requirements on the other.

It is impossible in this publication to exhaust the potentialities of these graphs: closer study will reveal many further refinements to those who are interested in personnel selection and classification problems. For example, it is possible to provide answers to the following type of question:

(a) What must be the battery cut-off score to ensure that virtually no failures (i.e. at the worst one failure in 100 selectees) are selected?

(b) What must be the battery cut-off score to ensure that virtually no successes are rejected?

The consequences of selection by an aptitude test battery are discussed at greater length in another publication by the author (1953), where certain laws of the operating characteristics are set out, and their implications considered for selection policy.

Table 29

CUT-OFF SCORE α		SELECTORS' OPERATING CHARACTERISTIC FIG. 3	MANAGEMENT'S OPERATING CHARACTERISTICS FIG. 7						FIG. 9		FIG. 10
			Percentage of Applicant Population						Percentage of Selectees who are successes		
Standard Measures	Standard Scores	Probability of success at this level [β = 0·643 S.M.]	Rejected and Failures	Rejected and Successes	Total Rejected	Selected and Failures	Selected and Successes	Total Selected	Battery Selection r = 0·68	Select'n by Technique r = 0	Efficiency Index (H₁)
−1·0	40	0·04 or 4 in 100	15·5	0·0	15·5	58·5	26·0	84·5	30·6	26·0	4·6%
−0·5	45	0·09 or 9 in 100	29·7	1·3	31·0	44·3	24·7	69·0	35·9	26·0	9·9%
0	50	0·19 or 19 in 100	46·2	3·8	50·0	27·8	22·2	50·0	44·5	26·0	18·5%
+0·5	55	0·34 or 34 in 100	60·5	8·7	69·2	13·4	17·4	30·8	55·9	26·0	29·9%
+1·0	60	0·51 or 51 in 100	69·0	15·0	84·0	5·0	11·0	16·0	68·8	26·0	42·8%
+1·5	65	0·69 or 69 in 100	72·6	20·5	93·1	1·3	5·6	6·9	80·6	26·0	54·6%

CHAPTER VII

THE NET GAINS OF TEST BATTERY SELECTION

Comparison between battery selection and selection by board procedure

WHEN CONSIDERING THE definition given above of the efficiency index of the test battery, it might be justifiably argued that the alternative selection procedure which the organization would have adopted in the present circumstances (i.e. the use of a selection board) would not have had a zero correlation with the criterion, and that the efficiency index does not represent the true, or net, gain to the Corporation of the use of tests in place of the conventional method. The efficiency index given represents therefore the *maximum possible gains*. These might well be an exaggeration of the usefulness of test selection over normal procedures. This argument is readily conceded, but, for reasons already stated, it is difficult to say what would be the percentage of selectees who would be successes (P_1), or failures (π_1), under board procedures, *even supposing that their techniques were consistent.*

Clearly what is needed is to establish the coefficient of correlation between selection by board and the criterion of success.

In this instance we have no way of telling what the value of the correlation coefficient (r) for the board would be. This could only be established by research methods on rigorously controlled lines.

Some indication of the outcome can be given by comparing the results from another field. It is impossible here to give precise details of the field of operation, and the selection board procedures used without revealing the identity of the N.I.P.R.'s sponsor organization. It is only possible to state that candidates were being selected for supervisory roles where personality qualities of leadership were of major importance, in addition to potential ability for the type of work. Furthermore, selection in this instance was being undertaken by a board of experts, who were supposed to be thoroughly experienced and acquainted with all the operational demands and requirements of successful candidates. The board procedure consisted of:

(a) examination of letters of application, supported by testimonials and accompanying documents;

(b) biographical data considered to be relevant;

(c) interview by selection board.

The candidates selected by this method proceeded to a two years' training programme at the end of which formal examinations were written. These constituted the basis upon which candidates were either passed or failed. The examining authorities were independent of the selection board. The results of these selection procedures were submitted to the N.I.P.R. for analysis. The following information was provided:

(a) The total number of applicants.

(b) The total number of candidates selected.

(c) The final number of candidates who passed the examinations.

(d) The final number of candidates who failed the examinations.

A later follow-up study of the original data by Sichel and Maritz (1950) showed that it would not have been unreasonable to place the β value at -0.7 standard measures.

The above information yielded values for—

    (i) the cut-off point or select-reject dividing line (a);

    (ii) the success-failure dividing line (β);

    (iii) P_1 — the proportion of selectees who were successful.

The importance of these data can be appreciated by reference to Fig. 5.

Assuming the bivariate distribution to have been normal, and given the values for a, β, and P_1, the process somewhat resembles that used in reconstructing a prehistoric animal from a few bones. In this case the rest of the figure can be drawn up to reveal what the corresponding correlation coefficient (r) would be in order that the given results would follow. (See Appendix, section 7.)

With a training wastage in the present instance of 18%, the value of the correlation coefficient was found to be $r = 0.2$. This is merely the overall indication of the selecting efficiency achieved by this selection board method.

On the assumption that a selection board constituted at the Corporation would have been no more, but no less, efficient in the job of evaluating human material than the one referred to above, with $\beta = 0.643$, $r = 0.2$ and $a =$ various values, we can draw up a series of graphs representing the operating characteristics of the selection board technique, similar to those given for the present test battery. The appropriate curves are shown in Figures 10 to 13. A detailed study of these in comparison with their corresponding curves for test battery selection is an interesting exercise. In terms of these results the actual, or net, gains in efficiency to the Corporation resulting from the use of the test battery in place of conventional selection by a board, would be represented as:

$$(H_1) = \begin{bmatrix} P_1 \\ \text{(Test Battery} \\ \text{where } r = \cdot 68) \end{bmatrix} - \begin{bmatrix} P_1 \\ \text{(Selection Board} \\ \text{where } r = \cdot 2 \text{)} \end{bmatrix}$$

The significant findings for our particular purpose are summarized in Table 30 below. In this case we have placed the a value at $+1.7$ (or 67 standard scores) for this is the cut-off score which is most likely to be adopted in practice.

Table 30

| Selection Method | Percentage of Applicant Population | | | | | | P_1 | H_1 |
| | SELECTED | | | REJECTED | | | | |
	Failures	Successes	Total	Failures	Successes	Total		
Test Battery ($r = 0.68$) Figure 6	0·683	3·773	4·456	73·301	22·243	95·544	84·672	58·656
Selection Board ($r = 0.2$) Figure 12	2·624	1·832	4·456	71·360	24·184	95·544	41·113	15·097

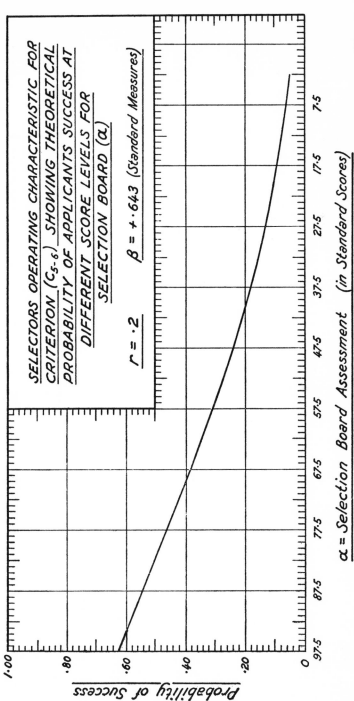

SELECTORS OPERATING CHARACTERISTIC FOR
CRITERION (C₅₋₆) SHOWING THEORETICAL
PROBABILITY OF APPLICANTS SUCCESS AT
DIFFERENT SCORE LEVELS FOR
SELECTION BOARD (α)

$r = \cdot 2$ $\beta = +\cdot 643$ (Standard Measures)

α = Selection Board Assessment (in Standard Scores)

Probability of Success

FIG. 10

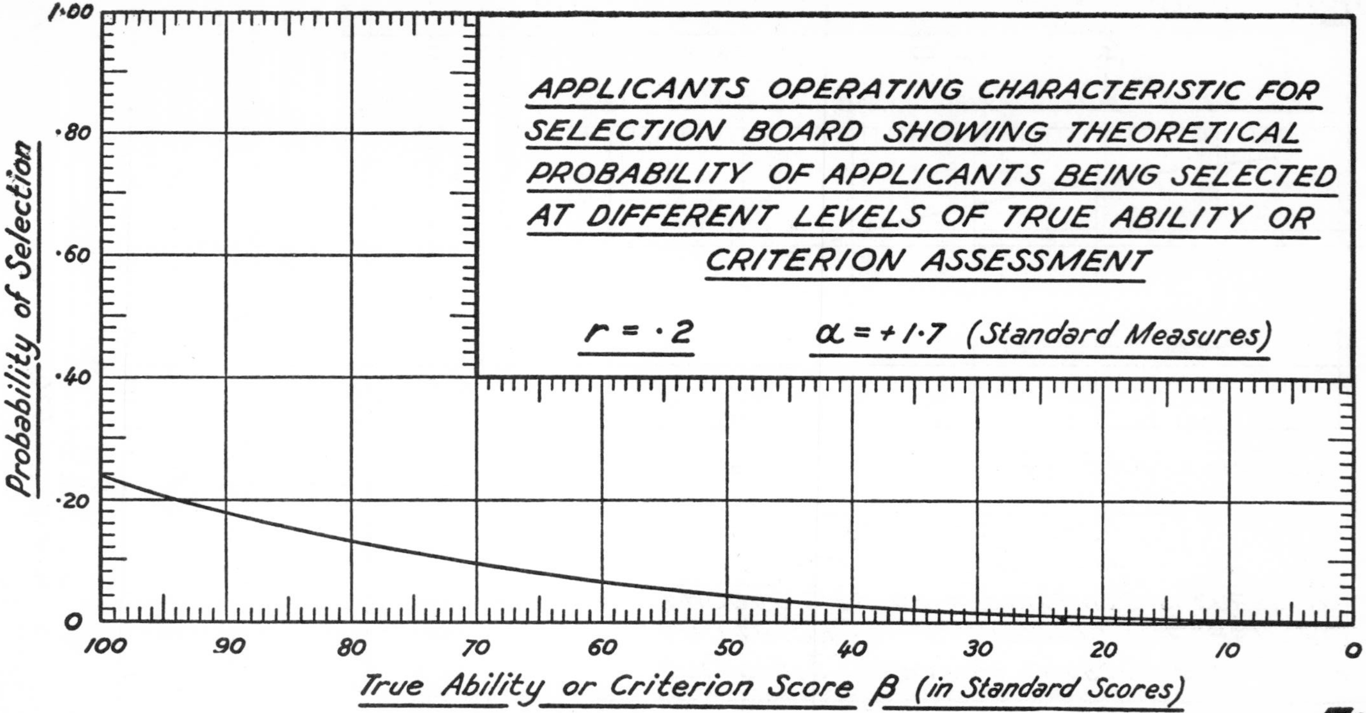
APPLICANTS OPERATING CHARACTERISTIC FOR SELECTION BOARD SHOWING THEORETICAL PROBABILITY OF APPLICANTS BEING SELECTED AT DIFFERENT LEVELS OF TRUE ABILITY OR CRITERION ASSESSMENT
r = ·2
α = +1·7 (Standard Measures)
Probability of Selection
1·00
·80
·60
·40
·20
0
100
90
80
70
60
50
40
30
20
10
0
True Ability or Criterion Score β (in Standard Scores)

FIG. 11

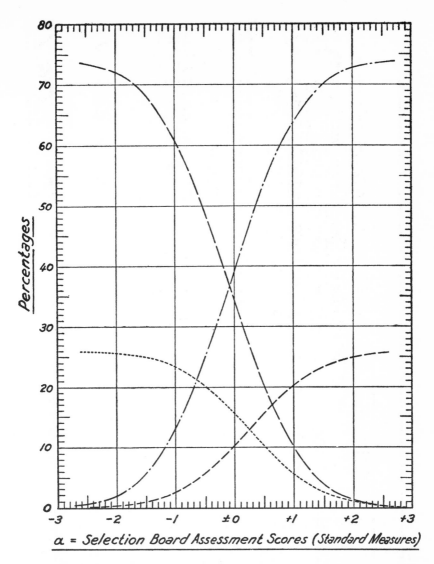

α = Selection Board Assessment Scores (Standard Measures)

GRAPHS SHOWING PERCENTAGES OF TOTAL POPULATION

1. Who are selected and successes ··················
2. „   „   „   „ failures —— —— ——
3. „   „ rejected „ successes —— —— —— ——
4. „   „   „   „ failures —·——·——·——

At different values of Selection Board Cut-off Score (α)

where { r = ·2
        β = + ·643 (Standard Measures)

FIG. 12

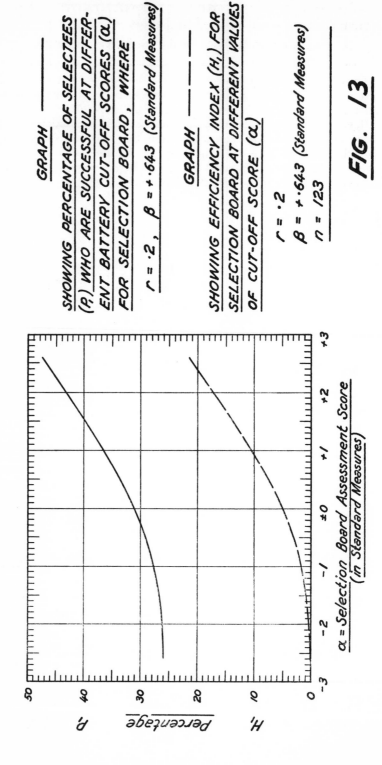

GRAPH ———

SHOWING PERCENTAGE OF SELECTEES (P₁) WHO ARE SUCCESSFUL AT DIFFERENT BATTERY CUT-OFF SCORES (α) FOR SELECTION BOARD, WHERE

$r = \cdot 2$, $\quad \beta = + \cdot 643$ (Standard Measures)

GRAPH — — —

SHOWING EFFICIENCY INDEX (H₁) FOR SELECTION BOARD AT DIFFERENT VALUES OF CUT-OFF SCORE (α)

$r = \cdot 2$
$\beta = + \cdot 643$ (Standard Measures)
$n = 123$

FIG. 13

From this table it will be observed that:

(i) (H_1) or efficiency index for the test battery = 58·656.

(ii) (H_1) or efficiency index for the selection board = 15·097.

Thus the net gain to the Corporation by using the test battery technique over selection board (assuming this board to be as efficient as was the other board of experts) is 58·656% − 15·097% = 43·559.

If, for the sake of argument, we assume that the Corporation's selection board was more efficient than the previous one referred to (e.g. $r = 0·4$ instead of 0·2), then the net gain of the test battery would be 29·056%, which is still quite an appreciable amount when the serious consequences of mis-selection are taken into consideration.

CHAPTER VIII

WIDER APPLICATION OF THE TEST BATTERY

THE APPLICATION OF the test battery to the specific needs of selecting a limited number of administrative trainees has now been fully explained. Its potentialities have by no means been exhausted, and in this chapter we shall consider to what other purposes it can be profitably applied. Two general sets of circumstances will be discussed here.

(1) *Simple Twofold Classification*

Under the previous definition of efficiency, management was only concerned with one source of error in the selection programme, viz. the proportion of selectees who turned out to be failures. Its concern was to reduce this percentage (π_1) (shaded area AEC in Fig. 14). As long as these requirements were being met management would be satisfied, and would not be worried about the proportion of rejectees who could be successful (shaded area DEB in Fig. 14), provided the requisite number of successful candidates were being selected. In other words the other source of error previously referred to in Chapter VII was really of no concern to management in that particular selection situation. It is conceivable, however, that these circumstances might easily change in such a way that the source of error associated with the number of rejectees who could make a success was of considerable importance to the selecting authorities.

Generally speaking, the reduction of the latter source of error may be regarded as a social objective of scientific selection, for it means that one would reduce the number of occasions on which a good man was denied his chance of advancement or making a success. However, circumstances may well arise where managements' interests are not antipathetic to social interests, and indeed may be mutually compatible with them. For example, where management wishes to make maximum use of its labour potential, by ensuring that all existing employees who could be elevated to more responsible work are in fact being given the necessary training and opportunity to do so, then it is important to consider the proportion of rejectees who could be successful, in addition to the proportion of selectees who would be failures.

The same considerations apply where labour is scarce and all available candidates have to be taken. Here it is important to ensure that all individuals who could be utilized for senior work are in fact recognized and appropriately graded.

In such circumstances as the above, it is not a question of shifting one's interest from the one source of error in selection to the other, but of taking the second into consideration together with the first. By so doing certain fundamental changes occur in the operating characteristics of the selection procedure, and the basic definition of selecting efficiency is altered.

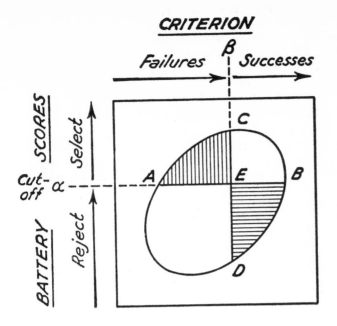

CRITERION

Failures — Successes

Area AEC ▥ represents candidates who are Selected and are Failures.

Area BED ▤ represents candidates who are Rejected and are Successes.

Area CEB represents candidates who are Selected and are Successes.

Area AED represents candidates who are Rejected and are Failures

FIG.14 SHOWING SELECTION AND REJECTION OF SUCCESSES AND FAILURES ACCORDING TO THE NORMAL BIVARIATE SURFACE FOR CORRELATION, AT BATTERY CUT-OFF SCORE (α)

FIG. 14

Under the new demands of the selection programme the operating characteristics of our test battery become as follows:

(a) Fig. 2—selector's operating characteristic ⎫
(b) Fig. 3—applicant's operating characteristic ⎬ remain the same.
(c) Fig. 6—management's operating characteristic ⎭

(d) Fig. 8—showing the graphs for values of P_1, has now to be replaced by Fig. 15 for P_2, where

$$P_2 = \frac{(\text{No. of successes selected} + \text{No. of failures rejected}) \times 100}{\text{Total candidate population}}$$

$$= \frac{\text{CEB} + \text{AED}}{\text{AEC} + \text{CEB} + \text{BED} + \text{AED}}$$

This then represents the percentage of correct decisions, or placements resulting from selection.

(e) Fig. 9—the graph of the efficiency index (H_1) is now discarded.

As the result of the above changes certain explanatory comments are called for.

(a) As the cut-off score (a) is raised for the test battery $(r = 0.68)$ the values of P_1 and P_2 both rise rapidly, but in the case of the latter this rise is not maintained after a certain point. Thus, under those conditions where one is forced to consider in addition to the failures who were selected, the percentage of rejectees who could have made a success, then there is definitely an *optimum cut-off point**** at which the test battery achieves its maximum percentage of correct placements (P_2). In this particular instance the cut-off score is at $a =$ approx. 1.0, or a standard score of 60. It can be shown that this optimum point of a for any test battery is $= \dfrac{\beta}{r}$. (See Appendix, section 8.)

(b) It is now no longer possible to define the efficiency of the test battery in terms of any specific index, as was done in the previous instance in terms of Sichel's definition of (H_1). It is conceivable that some case could be made out for using the gain in the *percentage of correct decisions* (P_2) as a basis for some quantitative definition, as P_1 was used formerly. The difficulty is, however, that under the new set of conditions, one is dealing with *both*, instead of one source of error. Thus the converse percentage of mistakes or misfits is made up of:

(i) failures who are selected, and

(ii) successes who are rejected,

and these occur in different proportions at the various battery score levels. Thus it is possible for the percentage of mistakes to be the same at two different scores, but the proportions of the respective types of error to be entirely different, e.g.:

* For this concept the author is indebted to McClelland (1942).

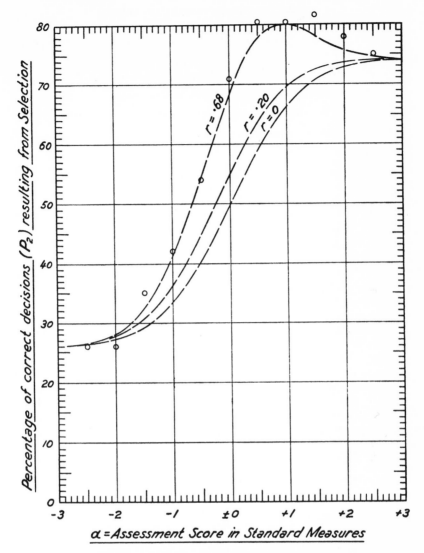

GRAPHS SHOWING PERCENTAGES OF CORRECT
DECISIONS IN TOTAL CANDIDATE GROUP (P₂)
AT VARIOUS ASSESSMENT SCORES (α) FOR

(a) Test Battery Selection, where r = ·68
(b) Selection by Technique, „ r = 0
(c) Board Selection, „ r = ·20

β = + ·643 (Standard Measures)

Observed percentages plotted by ○

FIG. 15

Table 31

FIGURE 7					FIGURE 17	
Battery Cut-off Score		Percentage of Candidate Population				
		Selected		Rejected		$\pi_2,\%$ of mistakes	P_2
a	BSS	Failure	Success	Failure	Success		
0·45	54·5	14·5	17·8	59·5	8·0	23%	77%
1·7	67	0·8	3·8	73·2	22·0	23%	77%

From Table 31 it will be seen that at 54·5 S.S. there are more failures selected, whereas at 67 S.S. there are more successes rejected.

Clearly, under certain circumstances it would be more serious to commit the one type of error rather than the other; and for other reasons stated elsewhere (Arbous, 1953) we cannot agree with McClelland's (1942) view that until some philosopher has assessed the relative importance of these errors in numerical terms, we are justified in assuming the two types of mistake to be equally harmful.

The concept must therefore be abandoned in favour of a more practical approach. Thus, given a certain manning problem, management is concerned to satisfy these requirements as best it can. Knowledge about the manner in which errors of selection behave will enable it to do so, by placing it in a position to evaluate the consequences of training wastage on the one hand, as against the shortage of competent staff on the other.

We should consider more specifically the answers to the following questions:

(i) In what percentage of the candidate population are correct decisions made (P_2) at the varying battery cut-off scores?

(ii) In what proportions do the two types of error occur at these levels?

If individuals scoring above the *optimum cut-off score* (60) are classified as administrative trainees, and those below it as 'non-administrative personnel', then Figure 15 indicates that management would be correct in $\pm 80\%$ of its decisions, and this is the maximum number of correct decisions which could be made on the basis of this test battery. If we were to raise or lower this cut-off score the percentage of correct decisions would be reduced.

The problem is, however, not simply that of establishing the optimum cut-off point for the test battery and then using that score level under all circumstances. The operating characteristics of the battery enable one to deal more skilfully with the situation where pros and cons have to be considered. This is best illustrated by placing the emphasis first on one, and then on the other conflicting need of the problem.

Let us examine the first proposition:

(a) *Management wants to reduce training wastage at all costs*

Under these circumstances the object will naturally be to set the cut-off score at such a point that the proportion of the population who are selected and failures is reduced to a minimum. What is the position at the optimum cut-off score of 60?

Table 32

Optimum Cut-off Score		Percentage of Candidate Population						P_2	H_1
		Selected			Rejected				
a	BSS	Failure	Success	Total	Failure	Success	Total		
+1·0	60	5	11	16	69	15	84	80%	43%

16% of the total population are selected in this case. 5% are selected and fail. The wastage rate is thus $\dfrac{5 \times 100}{16} = 31\%$. Because training may be expensive, this rate may be regarded as high. Management may thus decide that this should be reduced by 10%, i.e. to approximately 21%.

In order to achieve this, the cut-off score should be raised to 65 S.S. (Fig. 7) with the results as follows:

Table 33

New Cut-off Score		Percentage of Candidate Population						P_2	H_1
		Selected			Rejected				
a	BSS	Failure	Success	Total	Failure	Success	Total		
+1·5	65	1·5	5·5	7	72·5	20·5	93·0	78%	55%

The training wastage is now as desired, viz. $\dfrac{1·5 \times 100}{7} = \pm 21\%$. It will be noted, however, that this gain has been achieved at the expense of certain losses in other directions particularly with regard to the number of successes selected. In the given circumstances this will be deemed desirable.

The above selection policy would obviously apply in the case of Air Force pupil pilot selection, where training is expensive, and where failure could result in the loss of life of both pupil and instructor, or loss of aircraft valued at some thousands of pounds. It may well apply also in the case of administrative trainee selection.

On the other hand the need for trained staff may be so urgent that management may be forced to consider the proposition:

(b) *Every man counts, and the cost of training is a secondary consideration*

Under these conditions Table 32 shows that at the optimum cut-off score 11% of the population are selected and will be successful. However, at this level management is only utilizing $\dfrac{11 \times 100}{11 + 15} = \pm 42\%$ of potentially successful material in the population. This 11% may not be satisfying the manning requirements of the organization and a decision may be taken to the effect that selection should allow for the training of 77% (instead of 42%) of the potential successes. Accordingly Figure 6 shows that the battery cut-off score should be lowered to 52·5 S.S. with the following results:

Table 34

New Battery Cut-off Score		Percentage of Candidate Population						P_2	H_1
		Selected			Rejected				
a	BSS	Failure	Success	Total	Failure	Success	Total		
+0·25	52·5	20·0	20·0	40·0	54·0	6·0	60·0	74%	24%

At this level $\dfrac{20 \times 100}{20 + 6} = 77\%$ of the successes in the population have been selected. The cost in this case is to increase the training wastage which will be $\dfrac{20 \times 100}{40} = 50\%$ for which allowances must be made in the training programme.

In the above two propositions the emphasis was placed exclusively on each of the major demands in the selection programme. This was done principally for purposes of illustration. In actual practice many situations will arise where the choice between the two is not an all-or-none matter, but will depend upon a more subtle evaluation of the full consequences. The point, however, is that the operating characteristics given in the preceding figures provide management with a means whereby this can be done. The gains and losses of a selection programme can be blended in such a manner that they will satisfy the relative demands of training and manning policy.

In general, however, there is a point which it is important to bear in mind. Under many circumstances it must be considered more serious to select a failure than to reject a success, despite the fact that the degree of relationship cannot be expressed in quantitative terms. This is particularly applicable where a period of training does not intervene between selection and appointment to some job. A person can always be failed in an examination without much harm other than wasting the training. On the other hand, once an individual is placed in a post, it is often a very difficult problem to get rid of him, if he turns out to be a failure. Untold damage can follow over a period of years as the result of placing a 'small peg in a big hole'. Even if demotion or dismissal can be resorted to (supposing inefficiency can be proved beyond doubt), this is bound to be accompanied by some harm to group morale.

On the other hand, if a success is rejected at the time of selection, the individual (if he is a present employee) is not forgotten, but is followed up in his work. If he shows promise he can always be promoted at a later date, which is a far more desirable and happy remedy than demotion in the other case.

The above examples serve to illustrate that, when making any decisions, it is necessary to scrutinize very closely the appropriate graphs of the operating characteristics, which will show the pros and cons of any selection policy. There is nothing purely routine about the way cut-off points are to be determined, and the implications of any decision must be fully worked out in relation to the operating needs and circumstances of the existing situation. Failure to do this in advance may lead to serious disappointment in the net results of the selection programme. These comments apply even when the validity coefficient of the test battery is higher than 0·68. It can be shown that many surprises may follow ill-considered decisions, even supposing one is working under ideal conditions where the validity coefficient is 1·0 (i.e. unity, or theoretical perfection). As a matter of fact it is a strange paradox that the higher the final validity coefficient of the test battery, the more important it is to fix correctly the correct cut-off point on the battery score. These considerations have been elaborated in another publication (Arbous, 1953).

It is often considered in many quarters that, once an acceptable validity coefficient has been obtained for a test battery, its efficiency has been guaranteed for all time, and under all sets of circumstances. This belief rather presupposes that test battery selection works *in vacuo*, and that selection at one level of cut-off accomplishes just as much as at others.

It should be clear that the size of a validity coefficient by itself gives little indication of the practical usefulness of the battery to which it refers. This will depend as much on the circumstances under which it is to be used, and the particular managerial purpose which it is required to fulfil. The major advantage of the approach to validity in terms of operating characteristics is that it shows to what extent the test battery will enable management to formulate selection policies which will adjust operational demands in an efficient manner to available manpower resources.

(2) *The Classification of Clerical, Executive and Administrative Personnel*

In the previous section where we were concerned with both sources of error in selection, the case might conveniently have been regarded as the simplest form of classification of personnel into *two* categories—i.e. where the whole sample is taken into employment, or where one is dealing with the existing employee population, and it is principally a matter of deciding into which of the two following categories each individual should be classed:

    (*a*)   those to be trained and eligible for supervisory positions;

    (*b*)   those who are not.

We shall now consider the case where management is interested in making a threefold classification of its existing personnel in terms of potential ability, and by means of which each individual's occupational ceiling will be determined in the hierarchy of clerical-executive-administrative work.

The example of threefold classification will be given here primarily to illustrate the use to which the test battery can be put, and not to suggest what should happen in this particular situation. Where circumstances are such that a threefold classification scheme is necessary, then the following technique can be employed.

It is assumed, for example, that management wishes to classify the working population into three classes, as defined in Criterion 5 (see Annexure C):

(a) clerical,

(b) executive,

(c) administrative.

In terms of this programme it is necessary that a decision should be reached in respect of each employee, as to his suitability for duties under one of these respective headings. Such a classification, if it could be accurately made, would undoubtedly have the following advantages:

(a) that optimum use was being made of the group's potential ability;

(b) that no individual was operating above or below the level of his innate capacity to the detriment of both himself and of management.

Just how effective is the present test battery in accomplishing these ends? It will be remembered that the criterion assessment (C_{5+6}) resulted in a broad threefold division of the candidate group as follows:

Table 35

	No. of Cases	%
(a) Low . . .	47	38·2
(b) Average . .	44	35·8
(c) High . . .	32	26·0
	123	100·0

We shall take these classes to represent respectively:

(a) clerical
(b) executive   } as defined in Annexure C.
(c) administrative

This means that individuals classed as 'low' were regarded by the assessors as being suitable primarily for 'clerical' work, etc., etc. The assumption would appear to be a reasonable one.

It follows, however, that we are now concerned with two (instead of one) dividing lines (or β values) in the criterion, segregating the three groups.

Furthermore, if we assume that ability in this field of work is distributed in a fairly normal fashion in the population (as are other abilities) it is possible, in terms of the number of cases observed in each criterion group, to calculate where the actual values of the two β's fall on a normalized standard scale.

In this case we get:

$\beta_1 = \quad 0·643$ standard measures (as before).

$\beta_2 = \quad -0·300$ standard measures.

This would result in the following three classes:

Table 36

	Low (Clerical)	Average (Executive)	High (Administrative)
Class Interval in Standard Measures	Below -0.300	-0.300 to 0.643	Above 0.643
Class Interval in Standard Scores	0 to 47.00	47.00 to 56.43	56.43 to 100
Percentage of Total Population	38.2%	35.8%	26.0%

It follows moreover that in order to classify the population into three classes by means of test battery scores, we must also have two cut-off points (or a values) a_1 and a_2, such that we group:

(a)   as administrators, those whose battery scores were above a_1.

(b)   as executives, those whose battery scores were between a_1 and a_2.

(c)   as clerks, those whose battery scores were below a_2.

The effectiveness of such grouping in predicting the criterion classification of the population by means of test battery scores, can be simply illustrated by reference to the normal bivariate surface shown in Figure 16. Here the criterion scale shows what the correct classification should be, and the test battery scale what it would be, at the two hypothetical values of a_1 and a_2 shown. In this particular case the two values of β_1 and β_2 are fixed as given above, but those for a_1 and a_2 can be shifted up and down the scale at will. Furthermore, the shaded areas of the figure indicate which proportions of the test battery classifications would be correct, while the unshaded remaining portions of the ellipse indicate the proportion of errors or misplacements.

Thus:

(a)   indicates proportion of population correctly classified as administrative;

(b)   indicates proportion of population correctly classified as executive;

(c)   indicates proportion of population correctly classified as clerical.

From this we can conclude that $(a+b+c)$ is equal to the total correct classifications;

$$\text{or } P_3 \text{ which } = \frac{(a+b+c) \times 100}{\text{Total candidate population}}.$$

Conversely:

(d)   represents executive incorrectly classified as administrators;

(e)   represents clerks incorrectly classified as administrators;

(f)   represents clerks incorrectly classified as executives;

(g)   represents executives incorrectly classified as clerks;

(h)   represents administrators incorrectly classified as clerks;

(i)   represents administrators incorrectly classified as executives.

FIG. 16

SHOWING PROPORTIONS AND TYPE OF CORRECT AND INCORRECT CLASSIFICATIONS BY TEST BATTERY ACCORDING TO THE NORMAL BIVARIATE SURFACE, AT THE TWO CUT-OFF SCORES α_1 AND α_2

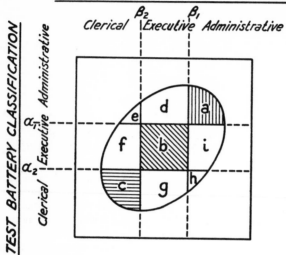

TRUE CLASSIFICATION BY CRITERION

TEST BATTERY CLASSIFICATION

I. CORRECT CLASSIFICATIONS.

Portion **a** represents true *Administrators* correctly classified as "

Portion **b** represents true *Executives* correctly classified as "

Portion **c** represents true *Clerks* correctly classified as "

II. ERRORS IN CLASSIFICATIONS

Portion **h** represents true *Administrators* incorrectly classified as *Clerks*.

Portion **i** represents true *Administrators* incorrectly classified as *Executives*.

Portion **d** represents true *Executives* incorrectly classified as *Administrators*.

Portion **g** represents true *Executives* incorrectly classified as *Clerks*.

Portion **e** represents true *Clerks* incorrectly classified as *Administrators*.

Portion **f** represents true *Clerks* incorrectly classified as *Executives*.

FIG. 16

7

Finally $(d+e+f+g+h+i)$ equals the total incorrect classifications or misfits.

In the case of the normal bivariate surface, all the above proportions can be calculated mathematically, and, as explained before, if our observed bivariate distribution can be reasonably accepted as normal, then the corresponding proportions for our particular test battery can be determined. From them the operating characteristics, as they apply to the problem of personnel classification into three classes, can be worked out.

The mathematics of this procedure, though fairly straightforward, are of a rather cumbersome nature, because the whole problem is complicated by two a, and two β, values. The reader will by now be acquainted with the underlying principles, and a detailed explanation is given in the Appendix, section 9.

Figs. 18 to 21 show, for our particular test battery ($r = 0.68$, $\beta_1 = 0.643$, $\beta_2 = -0.300$), and in terms of the criterion used (C_{5+6}), what the values of the proportions a, b, c . . . i are for different values of a_1 and a_2.

It is now merely necessary to calculate the actual values of P_3, as defined above, for all possible values of a_1 and a_2, and to illustrate what degree of success is being achieved by the present test battery.

The various values of P_3 have been graphed in Fig. 17 and the means by which this was constructed is simply explained as follows.

The lower cut-off point (a_2) is placed at a high level (as high as it is ever likely to be in practice) and the values of P_3 are then calculated for each value of a_1, up the scale above a_2. a_2 is then lowered a notch, and the same calculations are repeated for P_3, for the various ascending values of a_1. The process is repeated until a_2 has been placed at the lowest value. In such a way P_3 values are plotted for all possible a_1 values *for each* a_2. Obviously in each case a_1 can only be placed above a_2 to have any meaning, and that is why the graphs in Fig. 17 are of gradually increasing length, as the value of a_2 goes down the scale. Furthermore, in this case there is not one graph for the values of P_3 but a series, each showing the percentage of total correct classifications for all possible a_1 values, at each level of a_2. In this case we have only plotted graphs for certain values of a_2. There is no reason why intermediate values could not be used as well. Those chosen are sufficient for illustrative purposes.

The significant features to note about these graphs are:

(a) All show a hump at the value of approximately 0·75 for a_1. Thus, for any value of a_2 the P_3 value (or percentage of correct classifications) is at its maximum when $a_1 = 0.75$.

This is then the *optimum cut-off* point for a_1.

(b) As a_2 is brought down the scale its curve is situated uniformly at a higher level than the previous value for a_2. The highest curve is at approximately $a_2 = -0.5$, and below this value the whole curve drops for decreasing values of a_2.

The value of P_3, then, is at its maximum when $a_2 = -0.5$, and this is then the *optimum cut-off* point for a_2.

From these observations it will be concluded that, in the case of the present test battery, the highest percentage of correct classifications (P_3) is achieved when $a_1 = 0.75$ and $a_2 = -0.50$,

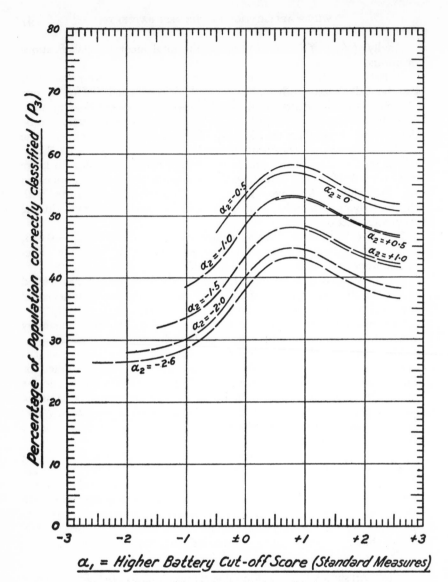

GRAPHS SHOWING PROPORTION OF TOTAL
POPULATION CORRECTLY CLASSIFIED (P_3) FOR
DIFFERENT BATTERY CUT-OFF SCORES α_1 AND α_2

$r = \cdot 68$
$\beta_1 = +\cdot 643$ (Standard Measures)
$\beta_2 = -\cdot 300$ „ „

FIG. 17

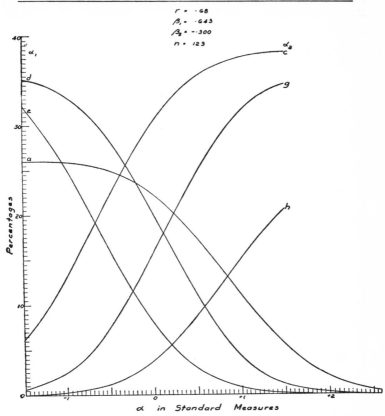

$$r = \cdot 68$$
$$\beta_1 = \cdot 643$$
$$\beta_2 = -\cdot 300$$
$$n = 123$$

α in Standard Measures

_N.B._ The various values of α apply to α$_1$ for a, d & e and α$_2$ for c, g & h.

For values of α$_1$
a = % of total population correctly classified as Administrators (A).
d = %   who are True Executives incorrectly classified as Administrators.
e = %   who are True Clerks incorrectly classified as Administrators.

For values of α$_2$
c = % of total population correctly classified as Clerks (C)
g = %   who are True Executives incorrectly classified as Clerks
h = %   who are True Administrators incorrectly classified as Clerks.

FIG. 18

GRAPHS OF MANAGEMENT'S OPERATING CHARACTERISTICS FOR CLASSIFICATION

IN TERMS OF TEST BATTERY SCORES AGAINST CRITERION C₅₊₆

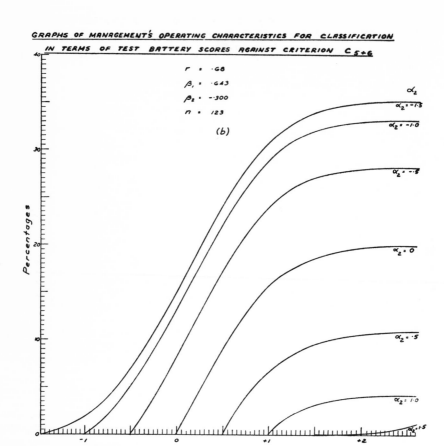

Graphs showing variations in 'b' for different values of α, and α₂

where b = % of Total Population who are correctly classified as Executives.

FIG. 19

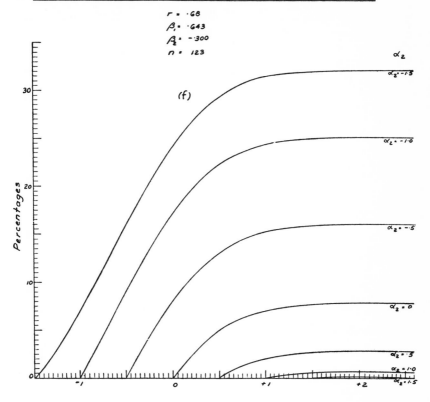

GRAPHS OF MANAGEMENT'S OPERATING CHARACTERISTICS FOR CLASSIFICATION
IN TERMS OF TEST BATTERY SCORES AGAINST CRITERION C_{5+6}

$r = \cdot 68$
$\beta_1 = \cdot 643$
$\beta_2 = -\cdot 300$
$n = 123$

α_2

$\alpha_2 = -\cdot 5$

(f)

$\alpha_2 = -1\cdot 0$

$\alpha_2 = -\cdot 5$

$\alpha_2 = 0$

$\alpha_2 = \cdot 5$

$\alpha_2 = 1\cdot 0$

$\alpha_2 = 1\cdot 5$

Percentages

α, in Standard Measures

Graphs showing variations in 'f' for different values of α, and α_2
where f = % of the Total Population who are True Clerks,
incorrectly classified as Executives.

FIG. 20

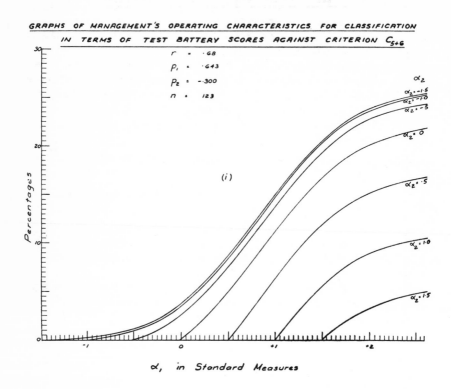

GRAPHS OF MANAGEMENT'S OPERATING CHARACTERISTICS FOR CLASSIFICATION
IN TERMS OF TEST BATTERY SCORES AGAINST CRITERION C_{5+6}

$r = \cdot 68$

$P_1 = \cdot 643$

$P_2 = -\cdot 300$

$n = 123$

Percentages

(i)

α, in Standard Measures

Graphs showing variations in 'i' for different values of α, and α_2
where $i = \%$ of Total Population who are True Administrators incorrectly
classified as Executives

FIG. 21

approximately. At these levels ±58% of the total population will be correctly classified in the clerical, executive, and administrative categories.

Again, it is impossible to evaluate this achievement by working out an efficiency index or (H) value which has any real meaning, as was done in the first case of pure selection. Whereas in the previous instance there were two types of error occurring in different proportions which precluded these estimations, there are now a maximum of six possible errors. Therefore the arguments used before now apply *a fortiori*.

It should however be obvious, even without some numerical index, that a method which enables one to see exactly what one is doing is superior to the orthodox procedure where there is no means of telling how one's classifications are going to work out.

There is a considerable practical advantage in being able to put questions like the following:

(*a*) What percentage of correct classifications is made in the various categories?

(*b*) What kinds of error are made, and in what proportions do they occur?

On the two previous occasions, when errors were being considered in this way, it was possible to illustrate the results by constructing simple graphs which showed variations in these errors, at all possible values of the cut-off score.

The series of graphs given in Figs. 18 to 21 provide management with a means whereby it can decide what classification policy to pursue in order to meet its particular manning requirements.

The crux of the practical problem is to decide what kind of selection error has most adverse consequences, and to take steps by means of which this error would be minimized. For example, it may be far less serious to classify an individual with executive ability as a clerk, than to classify a clerk, say, as an executive, or even as an administrator. Consequently it may be desirable to set the cut-off scores in such a way that many more of the former type of error are committed in order to reduce the incidence of the latter. It is imperative that the consequences of any decision should always be worked out and evaluated in this way.

At the two optimum values for a_1 and a_2 the following results are obtained in the sample followed up in this project (see Table 37). Thus:

(*a*) 38·2% of the total population have true ability qualifications for clerical work, and of these $\left(\dfrac{22 \cdot 2 \times 100}{38 \cdot 2}\right) = 58 \cdot 1\%$ are correctly classified as such, and $\left(\dfrac{16 \cdot 0 \times 100}{38 \cdot 2}\right) = 41 \cdot 9\%$ are not.

(*b*) 35·8% of the total population have true ability for executive work, and of these $\left(\dfrac{21 \cdot 4 \times 100}{35 \cdot 8}\right) = 59 \cdot 8\%$ are correctly classified while $\left(\dfrac{14 \cdot 4 \times 100}{35 \cdot 8}\right) = 40 \cdot 2\%$ are not.

Table 37

Groups to which Individuals Correctly Belong in Terms of Criterion	Percentage in Total Population at given value of $\beta_1 = +0.643$ $\beta_2 = -0.300$	Percentage of Total Population Classified at $a_1 = +0.75$, $a_2 = -0.50$				
		Correctly	Incorrectly			Total
			As Clerks	As Executive	As Admin.	
Clerical . . .	38.2%	c 22.2%	—	f 14.5%	e 1.5%	16.0%
Executive . .	35.8%	b 21.4%	g 7.4%	—	d 7.0%	14.4%
Administrative .	26.0%	a 14.5%	h 1.2%	i 10.3%	—	11.5%
	100.0%	58.1%	8.6%	24.8%	8.5%	41.9%

(c) 26% of the total population have true ability for administrative work, and of these $\left(\dfrac{14\cdot5 \times 100}{26\cdot0}\right) = 55\cdot8\%$ are correctly classified, while $\left(\dfrac{11\cdot5 \times 100}{26\cdot0}\right) = 44\cdot2\%$ are not.

These results show that the greatest percentage of correct classifications is achieved for executives; next the clerks, and finally the administrators. Furthermore, a study of the types of error committed indicates that:

(a) 14·5% of the total population are clerks incorrectly classified as executives;

(b) 1·5% of the total population are clerks incorrectly classified as administrators;

(c) 7·4% of the total population are executives incorrectly classified as clerks;

(d) 7·0% of the total population are executives incorrectly classified as administrators;

(e) 1·2% of the total population are administrators incorrectly classified as clerks;

(f) 10·3% of the total population are administrators incorrectly classified as executives.

Of the above (b) and (e) are the really serious errors, for they mean that individuals have been classified *two* grades above or below their true level. Fortunately they only amount to $(1\cdot5 + 1\cdot2) = 2\cdot7\%$ of the total population; i.e. serious errors of this nature would be committed in only three cases out of every 100 classified.

Errors (c) and (f) are not particularly serious for they mean that individuals are classified only one grade below their true level. These can easily be corrected later by promotion based on efficiency reports. In the meantime management will have the satisfaction of knowing that executive work is being efficiently done by some administrators (10·3%) and that clerical work is being efficiently done by some executives (7·4%).

Errors of this type will occur in 17·7% of the total cases classified.

The remaining types of error (a) and (d) are more serious than the last, though not quite as bad as the first. They consist of individuals being classified one grade above their true potential. Repercussions here can be quite serious, for as pointed out in an earlier section once the error has been committed the remedy is difficult, and if achieved by demotion usually results in unpleasantness. These errors occur in 21·5% of the total group classified.

The above facts explain the results of classification at the two cut-off scores used. Naturally before the programme is carried out management should evaluate these consequences in terms of manning requirements and the risks which it can afford to take in the various categories.

Furthermore, if it is desired, one cut-off level can be raised or lowered while the other is held constant, or both can be shifted up and down the scale at will. In each case a table similar to that given above should be constructed, and the consequences closely studied. In such a way manage-

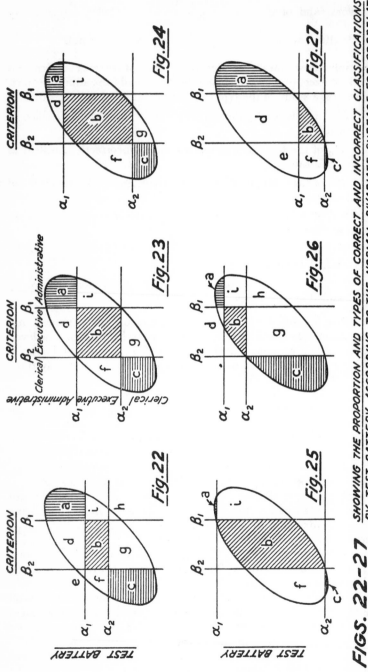

FIGS. 22-27 SHOWING THE PROPORTION AND TYPES OF CORRECT AND INCORRECT CLASSIFICATIONS BY TEST BATTERY ACCORDING TO THE NORMAL BIVARIATE SURFACE FOR CORRELATION AS THE CUT-OFF SCORES α_i AND α_2 ARE PLACED AT DIFFERENT LEVELS (For Legend see Fig.16)

The values for β_i and β_2 remain constant and are set by the criterion.

ment will be able to work out in advance the best solution to its particular manning problems.

A diagrammatic representation of the consequences of shifting the cut-off points a_1 and a_2 is given in Figs. 22 to 27. In the figures the shaded portions show the proportions of clerks, executives and administrators correctly classified, and the letters (d), (e), (f), (g), (h) and (i) show the proportions in which the different types of error occur in the total population. These diagrams are representative of only some of the changes which can occur when the cut-off levels are altered. They by no means exhaust the possibilities. Furthermore, the changes shown have been exaggerated in some cases for illustrative purposes.

In studying these figures, one should notice in particular how the proportions of clerks, executives and administrators who are correctly classified alter under the changing circumstances, and also how the respective proportions of the types of error vary, and in some cases actually disappear.

Thus for example in Fig. 24:

    (i)   comparatively few administrators are correctly classified, and the majority of them (errors (i)) are graded as executives; none, however (error (h)), is graded as a clerk;

    (ii)   the majority of executives are correctly classified, and errors (d) and (g) are small;

    (iii)   about half the clerks are properly classified, and errors (f) are fairly large, although none (error (e)) is graded as high as an administrator.

The above result would follow if one wanted a few successful administrators, many successful executives, and a fair amount only of clerks, and placed the cut-off scores a_1 and a_2 in the positions shown.

In all the above cases the corresponding graphs give the actual values of all the respective proportions shown. It will be appreciated, therefore, that once more management would be able to deal psychometrically with any classification programme, in such a way that the results could be planned in advance to meet its particular needs. Again, though the achievements of test battery classification cannot be stated in terms of any efficiency index, and even if one does not consider the gains to be highly significant, then at least it will be conceded that the degree of inefficiency of the technique is known, and management can plan accordingly and anticipate consequences, which no other technique enables it to do.

CHAPTER IX

THE SCREENING OF APPLICANTS

THE FULL USES and advantages of selection and/or classification by means of the present test battery have now been illustrated. Naturally when evaluating the gains to be achieved by the improved method it is necessary to weigh, on the one hand, the increase in the number of correct decisions in a situation where the consequences of mis-selection are serious, against the additional administrative cost of operating a test battery of this nature. The expenses here are obviously greater than those that would be incurred were the conventional selection board procedure to be used, where candidates are required to be present for a maximum of about half an hour each, or can be interviewed by representatives at local centres.

Before the final evaluation of the usefulness of the test battery is made along these lines, it is necessary to consider first what economies can be effected by means of screening devices, whereby a certain proportion of the applicant population can be eliminated in the first instance by means of relatively simple and inexpensive procedures. Thus, considerable saving in time and money could be effected by sparing selectors the trouble of testing by elaborate techniques those who have no chance of succeeding in administrative work.

The objects of the screening process can, therefore, be briefly stated as follows:

(a) To reduce the cost of testing by eliminating in the first instance those candidates who have *little or no chance* of obtaining the qualifying mark for selection (a).

(b) At the same time pre-screening should ensure that final selection will be no less efficient than it would have been had all applicants passed through the full testing procedures.

Thus, from management's point of view we should ensure that no good material is being lost in the screening process; and from the candidate's point of view that no individual is discriminated against by being rejected on the basis of one short test, and so prevented from improving his assessment by means of a full testing programme.

Clearly perfection can never be achieved in the assessment of human material, and it is impossible ever to be certain that absolutely no good material will be lost or that absolutely none will be unjustly rejected. It is possible, however, to set screening standards in such a way that one approaches very closely to these desirable objectives. In screening one is chiefly concerned with one type of error, viz. the rejection of those who would make the final battery score at which management will ultimately select after complete testing. This is usually decided upon in advance. Here the interests of management and the candidate are identical, and if the margin of error in this regard can be reduced to a minimum both parties should be satisfied.

To define quite specifically the operative words '*little or no chance*' in paragraph (*a*) above, we shall fix the basic condition under which screening is permissible as follows.

The cut-off score (γ) on the screening test shall be set in such a way that *at that level* the candidate has a probability of 0·01 of obtaining or surpassing the final battery score (*a*) at which management has decided selection will ultimately take place. This condition can be more concisely stated as:

$$p\ [x \geqslant a \mid \gamma] = 0·01$$

which merely equates to 0·01, the probability defined in Sichel's (1950 *b*) formula for the selector's operating characteristic, allowing for the necessary change in terms. (See Appendix, section 6.)*

This decision would mean in effect that the only candidates who are screened out are those whose chances are less than 1 in 100 of making the pre-determined battery score (*a*) when fully tested. It will be demonstrated that this safeguard against discrimination is adequate, and that no reasonable person should quibble at this small risk of error.

One further point must be considered in regard to this basic condition. We have spoken of the battery score at which management has decided to make final selection (*a*). This is neither a constant level for all batteries nor for the same battery on all occasions. It will vary according to selection policy (selection ratio). This in turn will depend upon the balance to be maintained between manning requirements, on the one hand, and training wastage on the other. The point is that for any given test battery these conditions of selection will be considered in advance, and the value of *a* will be known.

Thus to determine screening policy one should know:

(*a*) the total number of candidates from which selection must be made;

(*b*) the battery cut-off score which is going to be used to meet manning and training requirements. This can be determined by:

(i) knowing the number required for training; for example, Fig. 7 indicates that if sixteen are required, the battery cut-off score will be $a = +1·0$, or 60 S.S.;

or (ii) knowing the number of *successful* trainees required; for example, if five or six successes are required, Fig. 7 indicates that the final battery cut-off score to be used will be $a = 1·5$ or 65 S.S.;

or (iii) determining an *acceptable* standard for selection; for example, if it is accepted that any individual, whose probability of finally making a successful administrator is *at least* 0·5 (or 50 chances in 100) will be selected, then Fig. 3 indicates that the final battery score will be $a = +0·95$, or 59·5 S.S.

---

* In this particular case, where *y* is now the predictor variable and *x* the predicted, and where *a* and *β* have now to be replaced by *γ* and *a*, we may write:

$$p[x \geqslant a|\gamma] = \Phi\left(\frac{a - \rho y}{\sqrt{1 - \rho^2}}\right)$$

which, to fulfil our prescribed condition, we must equate to the value 0·01.

Once the policy has been set it becomes a matter of determining the efficiency with which the screening battery score can predict what the candidate's final battery score would be, if he were to go through the whole testing programme. From this an operating characteristic curve can be calculated, which will show at what screening test score the probability of reaching the desired battery score becomes 0·01, or similarly for any other margin of risk which one may decide to accept.

The process whereby these values are accurately estimated under all selection conditions is briefly as follows.

Two of the pencil-and-paper tests, which can be simply administered to groups, and which have high validity coefficients, are selected for screening purposes. In our particular case we have used tests A(F) and M (giving an assessment of the individual's general mental ability).

The efficiency of these tests by themselves in predicting the final battery score was estimated by correlation techniques to be:

Table 38

	A(F)	M	Final Battery Score
A(F)	—	·700	·805
M.		—	·626
Final Battery Score . .			—

Again, although the overlap between A(F) and M is high, the latter was retained, since a large discrepancy between scores on the two tests would indicate the necessity for retesting in the case of the one carrying the most weight.

From now on the process is exactly the same as that described in Chapter V, section 3: viz. given a set of intercorrelations such as the above, we can estimate with what weights A(F) and M must be combined to give maximum efficiency in predicting the final battery score.

The result is that when scores from A(F) and (M) are combined and weighted in the proportions 0·720 and 0·122 respectively, the predicting efficiency of the screening test is $r = 0·81$. This is high and satisfactory. On the basis of this result it is possible to calculate, for each screening test score, the probability of attaining a *given final* battery score, and to represent these in the form of a graph. This will then represent the selector's screening operating characteristic.

Whereas before we were using the final test battery score (α) to predict the *criterion* score (β), we are now using the screening test score (γ) to predict the final battery score (α) (which latter now becomes the predicted variable).

The underlying principles and mathematical method for estimating the probabilities are, however, fundamentally the same, and have already been illustrated in Chapter VI.

We shall give two examples here. It is assumed that under two different sets of conditions management's final selection policy is:

(a) There are 100 applicants, and ±7 trainees are finally required to be selected. This means that $\frac{7}{100}$ or 7% will be selected in the end and that, to achieve this, Fig. 6 indicates that the final battery cut-off score to be used is $a = 1.5$ or a B.S.S. of 65, for 7% of the candidates will fall at and above this level.

Under these circumstances it is necessary to set the screening test cut-off score (γ) in such a way that at this level a candidate's probability is 0·01 of attaining the final battery cut-off score of $a = 65$ S.S. The answer is given by Fig. 28 which indicates that this probability applies to a screening score of 51·5 (standard scores). In order to evaluate the consequences of this decision, it is necessary to work out precisely what will happen at this level. This can be done from the appropriate management screening operating characteristics. Fig. 29 indicates at all screening score levels the respective proportions of the applicant population who are *screened in*, and *out*, who *would* and *would not* make a final battery score of $a = 65$ S.S.

At a screening test cut-off score of $\gamma = 51.5$ S.S. the results are as follows:

Table 39

Screening Test Cut-off Score (γ)	PERCENTAGE OF APPLICANT POPULATION					
	Screened In			Screened Out		
	Would make B.S.S. 65	Would not make B.S.S. 65	Total	Would make B.S.S. 65	Would not make B.S.S. 65	Total
51·5 S.S.	6·587	37·451	44·038	0·094	55·868	55·962

In this table the proportion of candidates who would make the final battery score of 65 is 6·587% + 0·094% = 6·681%. Of this $\dfrac{0.094 \times 100}{6.681}$ or 1·4% are lost by being screened out. Therefore, the chances that management will lose good material in the screening process are extremely small.

While one should not depart from the agreed risk in screening, it is necessary at the same time to see what economies screening at this level has actually accomplished. The *total* columns show that approximately 56% of the applicants have been screened out, and approximately 44% in. Thus while preserving our conditional probability of 0·01, we have at the same time eliminated approximately 56% of the group.

Thus only 44%, instead of the total 100%, of the applicants will be required to go through the complete testing programme while at the same time only 1·4% (or in this case 0·094 of the total of 6·7 who would have made the final battery cut-off score of 65) are lost in the screening process.

A second example will illustrate the resulting economies still further.

(*b*) There are again 100 applicants, and management has decided that eleven *successful* trainees are required to fill posts (i.e. sixteen

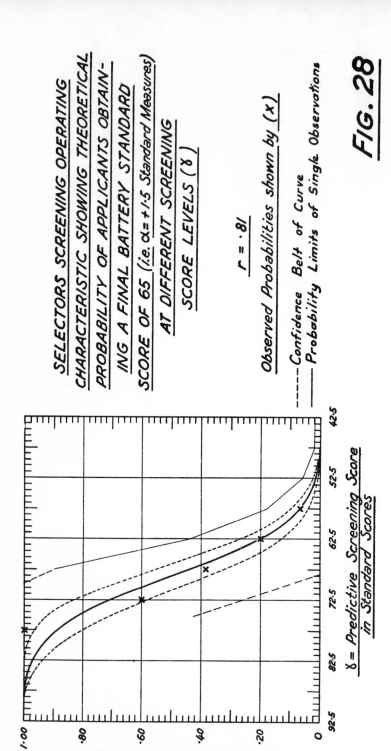

SELECTORS SCREENING OPERATING CHARACTERISTIC SHOWING THEORETICAL PROBABILITY OF APPLICANTS OBTAINING A FINAL BATTERY STANDARD SCORE OF 65 (i.e. $\alpha = +1.5$ Standard Measures) AT DIFFERENT SCREENING SCORE LEVELS (γ)

$r = .81$

Observed Probabilities shown by (x)

----- Confidence Belt of Curve
――― Probability Limits of Single Observations

FIG. 28

$\gamma =$ Predictive Screening Score in Standard Scores

Probability of obtaining Final Battery Standard Score of 65

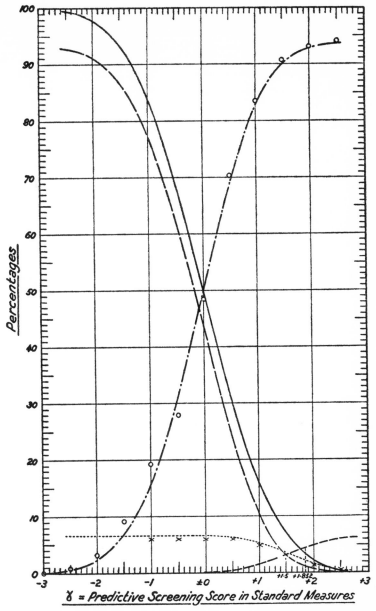

100

90

80

70

60

Percentages

50

40

30

20

10

0

-3   -2   -1   ±0   +1   +1·5 +1·852   +2   +3

γ = Predictive Screening Score in Standard Measures

GRAPHS SHOWING PROPORTIONS OF TOTAL POPULATION

1. Who are selected ————————————
2. „   „   „   and make Battery Score 65 ················
3. „   „   „   „   „ do not make „   „   65 ————————
4. „   „   rejected „ make Battery „   65 – – – – –
5. „   „   „   „ do not make „   „   65 —·—·—·—

At different Screening Cut-off Scores (γ)

r = ·81

Observed percentages plotted by o and x   FIG.29

will have to be selected). Thus Fig. 6 indicates that the final battery cut-off score which will be used is $a = 60$ S.S.

Under this selection policy a new set of graphs will be required to replace Fig. 28 and Fig. 29. These are given in Fig. 30 and Fig. 31, the former indicating that our screening test cut-off score is now 45·5 S.S., the latter showing the following screening results:

Table 40

Screening Tests Cut-off Score (γ)	PERCENTAGE OF APPLICANT POPULATION					
	Screened In			Screened Out		
	Would make B.S.S. 60	Would not make B.S.S. 60	Total	Would make B.S.S. 60	Would not make B.S.S. 60	Total
45·5	15·782	51·582	67·364	0·084	32·552	32·636

In this case the proportion of candidates who would make the final battery score of 60 is $15·782 + 0·084 = 15·866\%$, and of these $\dfrac{0·084 \times 100}{15·866} = 0·529\%$, are lost in screening. This is even less than in the former case. Furthermore, in this instance only approximately 33% of the population are eliminated by the screening process. The saving in the number of candidates who have to go through the complete testing programme is, therefore, not so great.

In the two examples given above, it has been necessary to work out the selector's screening operating characteristic curves (Figs. 28 and 30) in order to determine the screening cut-off score at which the candidate's chances are 1 in 100 of obtaining the predetermined final battery selection score of 65 S.S. and 60 S.S. respectively. This is a rather laborious task. To facilitate matters in this regard Fig. 32 has been constructed which enables one to read off immediately what the correct screening cut-off score should be, for every different final battery score at which management may decide to select—while at the same time preserving the basic operative condition, that only those individuals are screened out whose chances are less than 1 in 100 of making the final battery score at which selection will take place. Thus, for example, if ultimate selection is to take place at a battery standard score of 65 (x-axis), the graph for 1% chance indicates that the screening cut-off score should be 51·5 (y-axis). For $a = 60$, the screening cut-off score (γ) would be 45·5. These correspond with the values already given. All other values can be as expeditiously determined. (See Appendix, section 10, in regard to the method for constructing Fig. 32.)

In this particular case, we have laid down the condition that the screening cut-off score should be set in such a way that the candidate has only one chance in 100, at this level, of obtaining the required final battery score. Management may, however, decide that this level of acceptance is too lenient, and that the minimum chances of 'making the grade' in final testing should be 5%. This decision should only be made in the light of

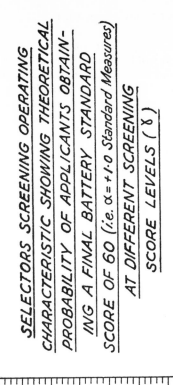

SELECTORS SCREENING OPERATING
CHARACTERISTIC SHOWING THEORETICAL
PROBABILITY OF APPLICANTS OBTAIN-
ING A FINAL BATTERY STANDARD
SCORE OF 60 (i.e. α = +1·0 Standard Measures)
AT DIFFERENT SCREENING
SCORE LEVELS (δ)

$$r = ·81$$

Observed Probabilities shown by (x)

----- Confidence Belt of Curve
——— Probability Limits of Single
      Observations

δ = Predictive Screening Score
    in Standard Scores

Probability of obtaining
Final Battery Standard Score of 60

FIG. 30

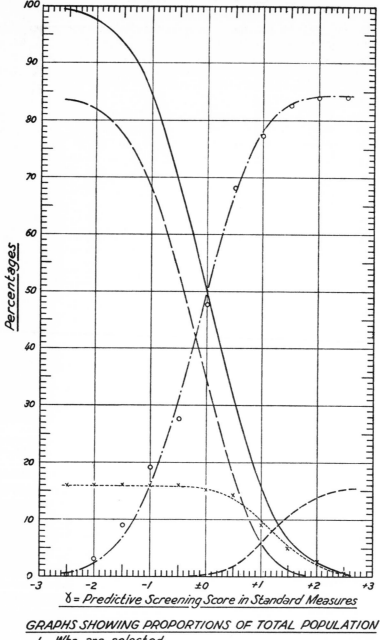

GRAPHS SHOWING PROPORTIONS OF TOTAL POPULATION

1. Who are selected ————
2. „ „ „ and make Battery Score 60 ············
3. „ „ „ „ do not make „ „ 60 —— ——
4. „ „ „ rejected „ make Battery „ 60 ———— ————
5. „ „ „ „ do not make „ „ 60 —·—·—

At different Screening Cut-off Scores (γ)

r = ·81

Observed percentages plotted by o and x   FIG. 31

information revealed from the set of operating characteristic curves given. Naturally, greater economies will be effected by screening at 5%, but at the same time the proportion of candidates making the final battery score, who will be lost in this process, will also increase slightly. These pros and cons should be carefully evaluated before policy is finally determined.

Under new conditions, if the chances are to be placed at the 5% instead of the 1% level, then the corresponding screening cut-off score can be ascertained from the second graph shown in Fig. 32. The following table gives a simple summary of the position for two battery scores:

Table 41

Final Battery Selection Score (a)	Screening Test Cut-off Score (γ)	Economies effected: % of population screened out	Losses: % of candidates who would make battery cut-off score, lost in screening process
65	(a) with 1% chance of making battery selection score = 51·5	56·0%	1·4%
	(b) with 5% chance of making battery selection score = 56·5	74·2%	8·0%
60	(a) With 1% chance of making battery selection score = 45·5	32·6%	0·5%
	(b) With 5% chance of making battery selection score = 50·5	52·0%	3·8%

The two examples given above are sufficient to illustrate certain important principles as regards the efficacy of screening:

  (a) The screening policy does not work *in vacuo*: it must be related to selection policy, which in turn is based on the training and manning requirements of the particular situation to be dealt with.

  (b) Acceptable risks of error in screening (viz. the elimination only of candidates whose probability is less than 0·01 or 0·05 of obtaining the final battery score at which selection will take place) must be agreed upon, and rigidly adhered to for all screening procedures.

  (c) To determine for $r = 0.81$, the precise screening test cut-off score to be used at the 1% or 5% confidence level, it is necessary merely to refer to Fig. 32. However, for each final battery score at which selection will ultimately take place, a new set of management's screening operating characteristic curves will have to be constructed, which will reveal the consequences of screening policy at both the 1% and 5% levels, in terms of:

  (i) economies which can be achieved;

  (ii) loss of eligible manpower in screening process.

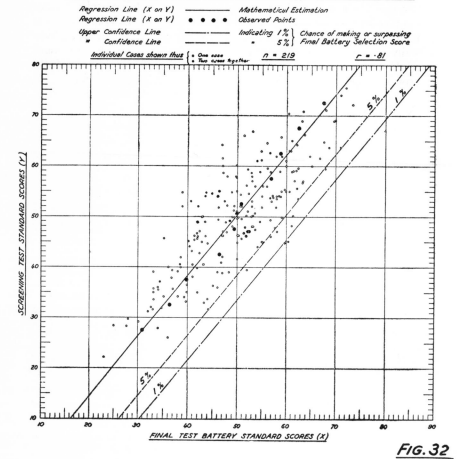

GRAPHS SHOWING SCREENING TEST STANDARD SCORES AT WHICH CANDIDATES HAVE 1% AND 5% CHANCE OF MAKING OR SURPASSING ANY GIVEN FINAL BATTERY SCORE AT WHICH SELECTION WILL ULTIMATELY TAKE PLACE

FIG. 32

(d) In general the graphs indicate that as more selected trainees are required, fewer applicants can be screened out, if the minimum acceptable probability of 0·01 or 0·05 be kept constant. The economies which can be achieved will therefore be less.

(e) At certain levels, i.e. if many or all *successes* in the population are required for training, the final battery selection score will be set very low. Screening may not be profitable at all, in view of the very small gains. Under these circumstances it is necessary to put *all* applicants through the full programme if one wants to reap a full harvest in the form of successful trainees.

It is important to note the extent to which our mathematical estimates are in fact a true representation of the observed facts. Evidence of this is to be found in Figs. 28, 30, and 32. In the former two, the probabilities actually observed in our data are reflected by crosses (x). The agreement between theory and observation is revealed by the manner in which these crosses straddle and approximate closely to the mathematical curves.

In Fig. 32 the agreement is even more strikingly revealed. Thus:

(a) The points of the observed regression line (0) lie very close to the line which was determined by mathematical estimation.

(b) Each small circle (o) represents one individual. There are 219 cases in all. According to mathematical theory:

(i) 1% of these should lie to the right of the 1% upper confidence line. In 219 cases there should be two or three. Inspection will show that there are in fact three observed points.

(ii) 5% should be to the right of the 5% upper confidence line. In 219 cases there should be approximately ten. There are in fact nine (with two additional points very close to the line).

Thus, without using more elaborate tests, the above observations should be convincing proof of the fact that the use of mathematical models to determine screening operating characteristics is quite a justifiable procedure, for the estimated results are in close agreement with the observed facts.

CHAPTER X

GENERAL COMMENTS

THE GENERAL VALIDITY and operating efficiency of the existing test battery have now been established and illustrated. Some general comments are however called for, lest it be assumed that from now on the application of this test battery is a simple, routine matter.

It is not suggested that the present battery is by any means the final answer to the problem of selecting and classifying clerical, executive and administrative personnel. There is room for considerable improvement.

(a) It has been shown that the efficiency of the battery depends on three factors:

  (i) the value of a, or battery cut-off score;

  (ii) the value of β, or success/failure dichotomy in the criterion;

  (iii) the value of r, or validity coefficient.

The first can be altered at will and can be so placed in terms of the operating characteristics that any given test battery can be made to do *its best* job under any given set of circumstances. However, this 'best job' is conditioned by the value of r. For any given a and β the higher the validity coefficient, the better will be the results of test battery selection or classification. It can be shown, for example, that if the r in our particular case could be raised from 0·68 to 0·80, the selecting efficiency (H_1) at the cut-off score $a = 67$ S.S. would be increased from approximately 58% to approximately 68%. In a similar manner the classifying efficiency of the battery would also be improved.

The validity coefficient r can, however, only be improved by further basic research. This should be directed along the following lines:

(1) *Improvement of Existing Tests*

This refers in particular to the trial interview, written project, final assessment on group test situations, and the clinical interview, since tests A(F) and M are standardized and should not be changed.

At present the clinical interview is retained in the test programme, because it is essential to obtain some explanation of the candidate's personality make-up. This procedure, in its present unstandardized form, cannot make a unique contribution to, nor be incorporated in the test battery in the sense that material from this source receives its appropriate weight in the final battery score. This is a major defect at present. It is recommended, therefore, that attempts should be made to analyse more thoroughly the information derived from this source, and so permit of a more comprehensive validation (under several headings) of the data obtained. This would allow personality factors to carry more weight than they do at present in the final battery score. For example, certain character defects, apparent in the clinical interview, might not easily be revealed in the group tests where personality assessments are made. The final battery score might well be high, indicating considerable aptitude for the work, but at the same time be an overestimate of the individual's true suitability. The fact that a candidate had left his previous employment under circumstances unfavourable to himself is a case in point. At present the clinical interview would serve as a safeguard against appointment in such a case.

However, as matters stand at present, to act on such information would have serious consequences for the whole selection programme. It would mean that selection was, in part, being determined by factors which are not incorporated in the final test battery score. The result would be to upset the whole psychometric structure of the operating characteristics, which depends entirely upon the validity coefficient ($r = 0.68$) between this score and the criterion of success. The need, therefore, for further research into the clinical interview becomes at once apparent and urgent. This will be considered more generally later.

As far as the trial interview, written project, and final group test assessments are concerned, it should not be forgotten that ratings in these tests are subjectively determined. Further research is, therefore, needed to standardize these tests in such a way that the reliability of judges and the standards of assessment are maintained, irrespective of time of testing, or changes in the identity of assessors. The manner in which improvements could be effected in the trial interview and group tests has been suggested by Pons (1951) and Arbous and Maree (1951), respectively.

(2) Validation of New Tests

The battery lacks at the moment standardized tests of language achievement (in both official languages) which will measure aptitude for secretarial as opposed to accounting work.

Furthermore, new tests should be devised which will give some assessment of temperament and personality make-up to supplement those already in use. For example, a quantitative method of assessing the results of the sociometric questionnaire constituted in a different form might well be considered here. The existing tests are not sufficient to cover this wide field, where so many factors have to be taken into consideration. Care should be taken to ensure that these new tests do not overlap with existing ones but make their own specific contribution, though small, to the assessment of these qualities.

(3) Improvement of Criterion

The reliability of the existing criterion (C_{5+6}) is estimated to be of the order of 0.84, and the validity of the test battery in predicting this is 0.68. By way of example it can be shown that, if our estimate of the reliability of the criterion be accurate, and if certain basic assumptions can be accepted, one can apply the correction formula suggested by Thorndike (1949, p. 107). This indicates that, had the criterion been 100% reliable then the validity of our battery might have been represented by a coefficient of $r = 0.74$.

Research should be directed, therefore, towards the improvement of the criterion itself, with particular reference to the discovery of more reliable, and perhaps objective, means of assessing 'success' in the administrative field.

Furthermore, another factor influencing the efficiency of test battery prediction is the point of demarcation (or β value) between success and failure in the criterion itself. In the present case it is $\beta = 0.643$ S.M. It is known that the operating characteristics of the battery will be materially changed if this point be shifted up or down. The writer (1953) has shown that for every given r and a there is an optimum point for β at which the test battery achieves its maximum efficiency. A study of the curves given in this publication shows that in the present instance with $a = 1.5$, $r = 0.68$ the given value of $\beta = 0.643$ is approximately at its optimum point. Consequently, if this value were raised or lowered the efficiency (H_1) of the test battery would decrease, and, as the values of r and a are high, fairly appreciable decreases would result from small changes in β. Are we justified in assuming that the present point is in fact the correct one? To what extent will changes in the nature of the work affect the proportion of individuals in the population who can make a success of it, thereby changing the true value of β? These aspects should be thoroughly investigated.

Finally, it cannot be too strongly emphasized that while the operating characteristics appear to give a very strict and precise picture of the workings of the present test battery, it must not be forgotten that these graphs only apply *provided certain conditions are maintained.*

These are chiefly:

(i) That the tests themselves are both administered and scored under highly standardized conditions. Anyone taking chances with these factors is likely to be gravely disappointed with the results, which will not turn out according to expectations. In particular it is necessary to refer to the need to standardize those test situations where subjective assessments are made (see paragraph (1) above).

Sichel (1948) has, by the application of statistical quality control techniques to test data, devised a method for determining whether test administration is being maintained within a state of statistical control. It was not possible to apply this technique in the present instance, but anyone using the battery on a routine basis would be strongly advised to introduce it.

(ii) That, on all subsequent occasions, each sample of candidates is representative of the original sample of 219, on the basis of which the present test battery has been validated.

Thus in the first selection programme there were some 529 effective letters of application. Of these, 361 were external, and 168 from employees within the Corporation's services. In view of management's decision that all internal applicants should be fully tested, and in order to keep the total number of testees within manageable proportions, a fairly strict standard was set in pre-screening the written letters of application of external candidates. Finally 219 individuals were fully tested of which the large majority (146) were employees of the Corporation. This then is the constitution of the first sample used for validation purposes, which, naturally, contained many individuals whose academic record may not have warranted their serious consideration as trainees.

Two changes took place in the second testing programme, for the next year:

(a) In view of the large number of internal employees previously tested, very few (six) applied on the second occasion.

(b) There were also fewer external applications (171) of whom approximately half (81) were accepted.

Consequently this second group of applicants contained none of that 'poorer' element which occurred in the first. It is impossible to gauge without a complete follow-up study what effect this would have on the operating characteristics drawn up on the basis of the original group.

(iii) A third condition is that the position of β should remain unchanged. Possible sources of variation here are:

(a) improved methods of training;

(b) simplification of the work due to studies of operational efficiency;

(c) the work increases in complexity due to new demands and/or the assigning of new responsibilities, duties, etc.

(iv) Selection is undertaken only on the basis of those variables which have been validated, weighted and incorporated into the final battery score. To select in terms of any additional extraneous factors such as age, experience, marital state, etc., when these have not been similarly validated, would upset the whole psychometric structure of the test battery.

(4) *Conclusion*

Lest the claims of the psychometric approach to personnel selection should appear to be overstated in this publication, it is essential that the technique should be compared with the more subjective assessment of test performance. The fundamental differences in methodological principle which become at once apparent will indicate the peculiar advantages and disadvantages of the two approaches, and point the need to future research whereby the basic difficulties should be resolved.

(a) *The subjective approach*

The individual or subjective approach to personnel selection rests on the belief that personality is too complex in its structure ever to be reducible to quantitative terms; that many attributes are not amenable to objective assessment. Reliance is, therefore, placed on the interview to pursue the pointers provided by various test procedures, to interpret these in the light of further information obtained from the clinical interview, and to arrive at a final appraisal of the personality which represents a synthesis of the available material.

This approach has the advantages:

(i) That use is made of additional material from the clinical interview.

(ii) That judgement is made in terms of the whole personality make-up.

(iii) That the technique is more readily comprehended by candidates.

(iv) That it can be more readily adapted to the changing demands of the training and man-power needs.

There are, however, equally severe disadvantages:

(i) The testing programme contains procedures that are not standardized, which means that consistent results cannot be guaranteed.

(ii) The efficacy of individual test procedures cannot be assessed.

(iii) Operating characteristics cannot be worked out which enable management to anticipate in advance the results of selection.

(iv) If the whole personality is to be appraised, a thoroughgoing psychiatric interview is required. This takes considerable time. If on the other hand, to save time, the clinical interview is superseded by biographical questionnaire data only, and these are to be handled psychometrically, the argument for the subjective approach falls away.

(b) *The psychometric approach*

The arguments for this approach can be deduced from the text of this book. To facilitate comparison they are briefly summarized as follows:

(i) The selecting inefficiency of the test battery is known, and suitable allowances can be made for errors of selection in advance.

(ii) Usually statistical quality control techniques can be applied to the test procedures to check the validity of the test, and determine the consistency of the battery's operating characteristics.

(iii) Personnel can be handled consistently in terms of predetermined operating characteristics.

(iv) Once the validation study has been carried out, and the operating characteristics and control charts determined, the testing procedure can be applied on a routine basis by assessors and testers who do not require the same degree of professional training in this work.

(v) As a result of (iv) large numbers of candidates can be handled by this method particularly with the aid of psychometric screening devices.

(vi) The procedures themselves allow for the setting-up of experimental conditions, and so facilitate research into new tests whose validity can be precisely and objectively determined.

(vii) Management is more likely to be interested in the psychometric approach because it enables one to plan and formulate training and manning policy in advance.

The following disadvantages should not, however, be overlooked:

(i) The technique is a very impersonal one—candidates may well feel that the opportunity has not been given them to plead their cases as effectively as they could have done in personal interviews. It is, moreover, doubtful whether an explanation of the applicant's operating characteristic will compensate for this: a mature and well-developed outlook is needed to comprehend this concept.

(ii) The method is limited by the number of objective techniques available for quantitative assessment. These are notably lacking in the field of personality studies. Here they are usually replaced by subjective rating scales of various types. These are universally known to be unreliable in their results unless highly skilled assessors are employed.

(iii) There are certain mathematical limitations. It is impossible under many circumstances to validate the procedures when the follow-up study can only be made on the restricted group of personnel selected.

(iv) The operating characteristics can only be applied to new groups of candidates when certain specific conditions mentioned above are maintained.

Should these conditions be violated the selector has no other alternative but to fall back on the subjective method of assessment.

The summaries given above of the various merits and demerits of the two approaches to personnel selection raise many problems of both an academic and practical nature, which can only be solved by further basic research.

APPENDIX

SECTION 1

A

Method adopted for inclusion of fifteen selected trainees on rating scale of Criterion 6

Table 16 on page 53 in the text gives the actual ratings of all assessors for each trainee. In order to calculate the mean rating it was necessary to determine numerical values for L, A, and H. This was done as follows.

These three ratings were regarded as class-intervals on the criterion scale into which the remaining 108 cases had been grouped by assessors in terms of the 'selection' process involved in C_6. The midpoints of these class-intervals were then determined by scaling the distribution in terms of the observed proportions. Thus, if we assume the attribute measured by the criterion to be normally distributed, we would expect the observed proportion $\left(\frac{23}{108} = 0.2130\right)$ of the group to fall within the sigma-scale range of $-\infty$ to -0.7961 sigma-units. The midpoint of this range was then regarded as the sigma-scale value of an L assessment. In a similar manner the midpoints of the A and H class-intervals could be determined.

The actual calculations are given in Table 42 (see facing page).

The numerical values of L, A, H were represented by the midpoints of the class-intervals (in sigma-scale units). These values were then substituted for the letters in Table 16, and the mean calculated for each trainee. Thus if the mean rating, e.g. $+0.953$, fell in the class interval $+0.7655$ to $+\infty$, this trainee was given an H assessment and would be grouped in that class for correlation purposes.

B

These considerations lead logically to *an explanation of the manner in which the product moment correlation coefficient (r) was calculated between the test scores and this criterion.* Again numerical values for L, A and H were required, and, by scaling, the midpoints of these class-intervals were determined in sigma-units in terms of the observed proportions which could be expected to fall under the normal distribution curve. In this case the calculated midpoints must change, for our sample n has now increased, by the inclusion of the fifteen trainees, to 123, and the proportions falling under L, A and H have altered.

The midpoints of the class-intervals of C_6 were thus determined as follows:

Table 43

	f	Acc. P	p	Ordinate	$\triangle$	Midpoints $\triangle/p$
L	23	0·1870	0·1870	0·2687	−0·2687	−1·4369
A	63	0·6992	0·5122	0·3482	−0·0795	−0·1552
H	37	1·0000	0·3008	0·0000	+0·3482	+1·1576

Weighted mean = +0·0049

Table 42

f	Accumulated Proportions P	Proportions p	Ordinate	$\triangle$	Mid-Points S-Units $\triangle/p$	Limits of Class Intervals in S-Units
L 23	0·2130	0·2130	0·2906	−0·2906	−1·3643	−∞ to −0·7961
A 61	0·7778	0·5648	0·2976	−0·0070	−0·0124	−0·7961 to +0·7655
H 24	1·0000	0·2222	0·0000	+0·2976	+1·3393	+0·7655 to +∞
108						

weighted mean = +0·0079

It will be appreciated that the process of scaling results in a normalization of the frequency distribution of 'scores' on the criterion variable.

From the above it will be noted that our correlation coefficient has been estimated by a triserial r, where the general formula for the multiserial coefficient is given by Jaspen* as :

$$r_{mult} = \frac{\sum_{i=1}^{k} (Z_{i-1} - Z_i)\bar{x}_i}{S_x \sum_{i=1}^{k} \frac{(Z_{i-1} - Z_i)^2}{P_i}} \qquad .. \qquad .. \qquad (1)$$

where k = number of classes into which the criterion is split.
  $\bar{x}_i$ = mean of the i-th array on the battery score scale.
  S_x = standard deviation of total battery score distribution.
  P_i = proportion of subject falling into the i-th criterion class.
  Z_i = normal ordinate associated with proportion:

$$P_i = \sum_{1}^{i} P_i.$$

For $k = 2$ formula (1) will after some algebra reduce to the biserial formula.

The premises on which multiserial r rests are:
  (i) the distribution of predictive scores must be continuous;
  (ii) the trait segmented into k categories must be continuous and
  (iii) must be normally distributed;
  (iv) the k segments must be adjacent;
  (v) the regression of the predictor on the segmented variable must be linear.

Conditions (i), (ii) and (iv) are usually met. Condition (iii) is violated in the case of a restricted group, which does not apply here. The question of rectilinearity of regression has been dealt with by Sichel (1950 b), who developed Jaspen's formula to the form:

$$r_{mult} = \frac{1}{S_y}\left(\frac{\Sigma xy}{NS_xS_y}\right) = \frac{1}{S_y}r \qquad .. \qquad .. \qquad (2)$$

which is the ordinary product moment coefficient corrected for coarse grouping by the factor S_y^{-1}.

Thus in our case the regression line has been plotted, not on the midpoints of the three classes as is usually the case, but against the actual mean values of the class as scaled off in terms of the normal integral. Of this formula (2) Sichel (1950 b) states: 'It follows that having worked out the correct midpoints of the criterion categories $\left(\frac{Z_{i-1} - Z_i}{P_i}\right)$, we may calculate the ordinary product moment correlation which we have to divide by the standard deviation of the segmented variable in order to allow for coarse grouping. Formula (1) is quicker for computational purposes, but (2), which of course leads to identical results with (1), ought to be used as it permits of plotting regression lines. Thus a multiserial r, with the exception of the trivial case of $k = 2$ (biserial), may be graphically tested for linearity.'

* Jaspen, (1946) *Psychometrika II*, 23–30.

SECTION 2

Technique used for combining assessments on C_5 with those on C_6

(i) It will be remembered that C_5 consisted of a nine-point scale, whereas C_6 had only three classes: L, A, and H.

(ii) C_5 was first reduced to a three-point scale by combining the three lowest, the three middle and the three highest classes of the nine-point scale, thus giving an L, A, and H grouping.

(iii) The midpoints of these class intervals of C_5 were then determined by scaling in the same manner as for C_6 (see Appendix, section 1). Thus:

Table 44

	f	Acc. P	p	Ordinate	$\triangle$	Mid-points $\triangle/p$
L	52	0·4228	0·4228	0·3915	−0·3915	−0·9260
A	57	0·4634	0·8862	0·1929	+0·1986	+0·4286
H	14	0·1138	1·0000	0·0000	+0·1929	+1·6951

Weighted mean $= +0.0096$

(iv) The values of L, A, and H for C_5 and C_6 are thus as follows in sigma-scale units:

	C_5	C_6
L	−0·9260	−1·4369
A	+0·4286	−0·1552
H	+1·6951	+1·1576

(v) In that these values are in terms of sigma-scale units, it is permissible to sum them to derive C_{5+6} for each individual. The possible combinations are given as follows:

Table 45

C_5	C_6	C_{5+6}
L	L	−2·3629
L	A	−1·0812
L	H	+0·2316
A	L	−1·0083
A	A	+0·2734
A	H	+1·5862
H	L	+0·2582
H	A	+1·5399
H	H	+2·8527

(vi) A frequency distribution of scores on C_{5+6} yielded the following:

Table 46

	Class	f	Grouping
L {	-2.3629	18	} 47
	-1.0812	29	
	-1.0083	5	
A {	$+0.2316$	5	
	$+0.2582$	0	} 44
	$+0.2734$	33	
	$+1.5399$	1	
H {	$+1.5862$	19	} 32
	$+2.8527$	13	
		$n = 123$	

(vii) The frequencies in the above table were arbitrarily grouped into forty-seven L's, forty-four A's and thirty-two H's. Again by the process of scaling referred to above, the midpoints of these classes were determined, and assigned as numerical values to L, A, and H for correlation purposes.

Thus:

Table 47

	f	Acc. P	p	Ordinate	$\triangle$	Midpoints $\triangle/p$	Limits of Class-intervals
L	47	0.3821	0.3821	0.3814	-0.3814	-0.9982	$-\infty$ to -0.300
A	44	0.7398	0.3577	0.3244	$+0.0570$	$+0.1594$	-0.300 to $+0.643$
H	32	1.0000	0.2602	0.0000	$+0.3244$	$+1.2467$	$+0.643$ to $+\infty$

weighted mean $= -0.0074$

(viii) For the purpose of calculating the product moment coefficient of correlation, the same formula was used as is given for C_6 in Appendix, section 1.

SECTION 3

Tests of significance of difference of the moment statistics of samples drawn without replacement from a finite population

Skellam (1949) gives the test as follows, where:

$$X \;=\; \text{variate values of total group}$$
$$x \;=\; \text{variate values of sample group}$$
$$F \;=\; \text{frequencies of total group}$$
$$f \;=\; \text{frequencies of sample group}$$
$$M_r \;=\; \Sigma\, X^r \;=\; \Sigma F d^r$$
$$S_r \;=\; \Sigma\, x^r \;=\; \Sigma f d^r$$

(*a*) For means:

$$E\,(S_1) \;=\; \frac{n}{N} \cdot M_1$$

$$E\,(S_1^2) \;=\; \frac{n\,(N-n)}{N\,(N-1)} \cdot M_2 + \frac{n\,(n-1)}{N\,(N-1)} \cdot M_1^2$$

$$\mathrm{var}\,(S_1) \;=\; E\,(S_1^2) - [\,E\,(S_1)\,]^2$$

$$\text{Observed } S_1 \;=\; \Sigma f d$$

$$\text{Critical ratio} \;=\; \frac{S_1 - E\,(S_1)}{\sqrt{\mathrm{var}\,(S_1)}}$$

(*b*) For standard deviations:

$$E\,(S_2) \;=\; \frac{n}{N} \cdot M_2$$

$$E\,(S_2^2) \;=\; \frac{n\,(N-n)}{N\,(N-1)} \cdot M_4 + \frac{n\,(n-1)}{N\,(N-1)} \cdot M_2^2$$

$$\mathrm{var}\,(S_2) \;=\; E\,(S_2^2) - [\,E\,(S_2)\,]^2$$

$$\text{Observed } S_2 \;=\; \Sigma f d^2$$

$$\text{Critical ratio} \;=\; \frac{S_2 - E\,(S_2)}{\sqrt{\mathrm{var}\,(S_2)}}$$

SECTION 5

Graphical Normalization of Battery Raw Scores

The battery raw scores in terms of C_{5+6} were normalized graphically by means of the following table:

Table 49

Highest Point of Class-interval (Raw Scores)	f	Cumulative Proportions	Probits × 10
85	1	99·99	—
80	4	99·54	76·04
75	6	97·72	69·95
70	3	94·98	66·45
65	17	93·61	65·22
60	30	85·84	60·71
55	40	72·15	55·89
50	51	53·88	50·98
45	41	30·59	44·93
40	21	11·87	38·20
35	3	2·28	30·05
30	2	0·91	26·34
	$n = 219$		

Values in column 4 were plotted against those in column 1 to give the graph in Fig. 33. From this the candidate's final battery standard score can be determined in terms of the battery raw score derived from the multiple regression equation given in the text.

TABLE 48

COMPARISON OF RESULTS OF SELECTION FOR C_3, C_4 AND C_{3+4}

	C_3	C_4	C_{3+4}
R_e	0·649 (S.E. = 0·050)	0·608 (S.E. = 0·057)	0·677 (S.E. = 0·049)
R_o	0·645	0·579	0·668
Test Weights	A(F) 0·158	A(F) 0·384	A(F) 0·225
	M 0·060	M —	M 0·064
	W.P. 0·302	W.P. 0·234	W.P. 0·239
	F.R. 0·190	F.R. 0·118	F.R. 0·309
	C.I. 0·096	C.I. —	C.I. —
β Value	+0·749 S.M.	+0·522 S.M.	+0·643 S.M.
P_1 at $\alpha = +1\cdot5$ (7%)	0·727	0·779	0·806
P_1 at $\alpha = +1\cdot0$ (16%)	0·582	0·678	0·688
H_1 at $\alpha = +1\cdot5$ (7%)	0·501	0·478	0·546
H_1 at $\alpha = +1\cdot0$ (16%)	0·356	0·377	0·428
Optimum α	+1·15 S.M.	+0·86 S.M.	+0·95 S.M.

Results of Selection at Optimum α

C_3

	Select			Reject			P_1	H_1	P_2
	F	S	Total	F	S	Total			
	0·044	0·081	0·125	0·730	0·145	0·875	0·651	0·424	0·811

C_4

	Select			Reject			P_1	H_1	P_2
	F	S	Total	F	S	Total			
	0·068	0·127	0·195	0·632	0·173	0·805	0·654	0·353	0·759

C_{3+4}

	Select			Reject			P_1	H_1	P_2
	F	S	Total	F	S	Total			
	0·056	0·115	0·171	0·684	0·145	0·829	0·673	0·413	0·799

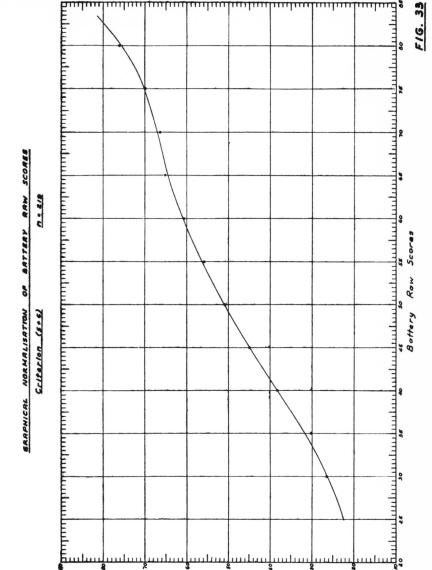

GRAPHICAL NORMALISATION OF BATTERY RAW SCORES

Criterion (5+6)   n = 818

Battery Raw Scores

Battery Standard Scores (Normalised)

FIG. 35

SECTION 6

Formulae for Selector's and Applicant's Operating Characteristics

(a)

Sichel (1950 *b*) gives the equation of the selector's operating characteristic in the case of a normal bivariate distribution as follows:

$$p(x) = \frac{1}{\sqrt{2\pi}} \int_{\frac{\beta - \rho x}{\sqrt{1-\rho^2}}}^{\infty} e^{-\frac{y^2}{2}} \, dy$$

which may be written more concisely as:

$$= \Phi\left(\frac{\beta - \rho x}{\sqrt{1 - \rho^2}}\right)$$

where $p(x) = $ probability of success for applicants of battery score x

$\beta \quad = $ boundary between success and failure on criterion scale in standard measures

$\rho \quad = $ correlation between battery scores and criterion

$x \quad = $ candidate's battery score in standard measures.

Substituting in the case of the present battery:

$r \quad = \quad 0\cdot68$

$\beta \quad = \quad 0\cdot643$

we have:

$$p(x) = \frac{1}{\sqrt{2\pi}} \int_{0\cdot87737 - 0\cdot92743x}^{\infty} e^{-\frac{y^2}{2}} \, dy$$

$$= \Phi\, (0\cdot87737 - 0\cdot92743\, x\,)$$

This equation was graphed in Fig. 2, for different values of x.

(b)

The equation of the applicant's operating characteristic for the case of a normal bivariate distribution is given as:

$$p(y) = \frac{1}{\sqrt{2\pi}} \int_{\frac{a-\rho y}{\sqrt{1-\rho^2}}}^{\infty} e^{-\frac{x^2}{2}} \, dx$$

or, more concisely:

$$p\,(y) = \Phi\left(\frac{a - \rho y}{\sqrt{1 - \rho^2}}\right)$$

where:

$p(y)$ = probability of applicant's selection for a given true ability (criterion) score

a = cut-off point of battery scale in standard measures

ρ = correlation between battery scores and criterion

y = applicant's true ability or criterion score in standard measures.

Substituting in the case of the present battery:

$$r = 0.68$$
$$a = 1.7$$

we have:

$$p(y) = \frac{1}{\sqrt{2\pi}} \int_{2.31857 - 0.92743y}^{\infty} e^{-\frac{x^2}{2}} dx$$

$$= \Phi(2.31857 - 0.92743\,y).$$

This equation was graphed in Fig. 3 for different values of y.

SECTION 7

Estimate of Validity Coefficient of Selection Board based on Selection Results

In this particular case the following data were ascertained from a follow-up study made by Sichel and Maritz (1950):

(i) Size of sample $n = 99$.

(ii) Number selected $= 36$, i.e. approximately 36%.
Hence had the selection board been selecting in terms of some scale represented in sigma-units, their cut-off point would have been $a = +0.33$.

(iii) The wastage rate for board selection was estimated to be 18% (i.e. percentage of selectees who turned out to be failures).

(iv) The pass-fail cut-off on the criterion was estimated to be $\beta = -0.70$.
The problem now is to estimate the r for the given a and β such that a wastage rate of 18% will result.

(i.e. $\dfrac{\text{AEC}}{\text{ACB}}$ in Fig. 14 $= 18\%$).

This was done by approximation and subsequent interpolation as follows:

First approximation:

$$\text{with} \quad a = 0.33$$
$$\beta = -0.70$$
$$\text{let} \quad r = 0.3 \,.$$

This yielded a wastage rate of 14.9501%.

Second approximation:

$$\text{with} \quad a = 0.33$$
$$\beta = -0.70$$
$$\text{let} \quad r = 0.1 \,.$$

Here the wastage rate is calculated to be 21.0602%.

By interpolating 18.0000 between 14.9501 and 21.0602 for the values of $r = 0.3$ and $r = 0.1$ respectively, the r applicable to our data was estimated to be $r = 0.2002$.

SECTION 8

Proof that the Optimum Point for $a_{y_0} = \beta/\rho$

McClelland (1942, p. 132) has already demonstrated that π_2 (i.e. portion AEC + DEB in Fig. 34) is at its minimum where the plane at a intersects the plane at β at the point where the latter intersects the regression line of x (the criterion) on y (test battery).

The mathematical proof of this has been given by A. S. Robertson (quoted by McClelland) by taking the expression for the sum of the volume AEC and DEB, differentiating, and equating to zero.

Since this is so, the value of β at which the plane CD intersects the regression line (RS) of x on y can be given by the following equation:

$$\beta = \rho \frac{\sigma_x}{\sigma_y}\left[a_{y_0} - \bar{y}\right] + \bar{x}.$$

This is a special case of the general equation of the regression line for x on y. As we are here dealing with normal marginal frequency distributions with the variables expressed in standard measures:

$$\sigma_x = 1$$
$$\sigma_y = 1$$
$$\bar{x} = 0$$
$$\bar{y} = 0$$

Then the equation above can be reduced to:

$$\beta = \rho a_{y_0}$$

whence,
$$a_{y_0} = \frac{\beta}{\rho}$$

Similarly, it can be shown that the optimum value for $\beta(\beta_{x_0})$, for any given battery cut-off score a, can be represented by:

$$\beta_{x_0} = \frac{a}{\rho}$$

DIAGRAM REPRESENTING THEORETICAL
BIVARIATE FREQUENCY DISTRIBUTION

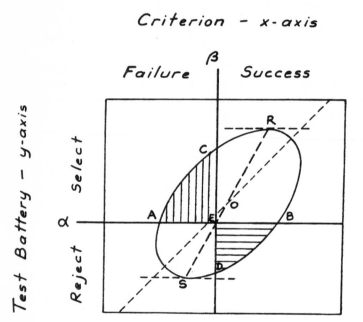

Criterion - x-axis

FIG. 34

SECTION 9

Method for Calculating Proportions of the Population Falling in the Areas a - i in Fig. 16

The method for determining the various proportions represented by the letters in Fig. 16 of the text is best illustrated as follows:

Let successes be represented by Su.

Let failures be represented by F.

Let selected be represented by S.

Let rejected be represented by R.

Then proportion $a = \text{Su} \mid \text{S}_{\alpha_1\beta_1}$

This is a convenient shorthand statement for 'the proportion a is equal to the proportion of the total population who are *successes, and who are selected* when the cut-off score is α_1 and the dichotomy on the criterion is placed at β_1.'

In a similar manner:

$$\text{proportion } b = \left[\text{Su} \mid \text{S}_{\alpha_2\beta_2} - \text{Su} \mid \text{S}_{\alpha_1\beta_2}\right] - \left[\text{Su} \mid \text{R}_{\alpha_1\beta_1} - \text{Su} \mid \text{R}_{\alpha_2\beta_1}\right]$$

$$\text{or } \left[\text{Su} \mid \text{S}_{\alpha_2\beta_2} - \text{Su} \mid \text{S}_{\alpha_2\beta_1}\right] - \left[\text{F} \mid \text{S}_{\alpha_1\beta_1} - \text{F} \mid \text{S}_{\alpha_1\beta_2}\right]$$

$$c = \text{F} \mid \text{R}_{\alpha_2\beta_2}$$

$$d = \text{F} \mid \text{S}_{\alpha_1\beta_1} - \text{F} \mid \text{S}_{\alpha_1\beta_2}$$

$$e = \text{F} \mid \text{S}_{\alpha_1\beta_2}$$

$$f = \text{F} \mid \text{S}_{\alpha_2\beta_2} - \text{F} \mid \text{S}_{\alpha_1\beta_2}$$

$$g = \text{Su} \mid \text{R}_{\alpha_2\beta_2} - \text{Su} \mid \text{R}_{\alpha_2\beta_1}$$

$$h = \text{Su} \mid \text{R}_{\alpha_2\beta_1}$$

$$i = \text{Su} \mid \text{R}_{\alpha_1\beta_1} - \text{Su} \mid \text{R}_{\alpha_2\beta_1}$$

It will be seen that all the proportions in the above equations can readily be ascertained by the method described in the text for Fig. 5, since in all cases:

Su | S is represented by CEB,

Su | R is represented by DEB,

F | S   is represented by AEC,

F | R   is represented by AED.

It is then merely a question of determining, by reference to Pearson's Tables (54), the appropriate values of CEB, DEB, AEC, AED, for the varying values of α_1 and α_2, β_1 and β_2 and inserting them in the above equations in order to calculate a, b, c, d, e, f, g, h, and i.

SECTION 10

Construction of Figure 32

The graph in Fig. 32 merely represents the theoretical regression line for the final test battery standard score (x) on the screening test standard score (y).

The equation to this is given as:

$$X = \frac{rS_X}{S_Y}(Y - \overline{Y}) + \overline{X} \qquad \cdots \qquad \cdots \qquad \cdots \qquad (1)$$

where
$Y =$ screening test raw score.
$X =$ test battery raw score.
$S_Y =$ standard deviation of Y scores.
$S_X =$ standard deviation of X scores.
$\overline{Y} =$ mean of Y scores.
$\overline{X} =$ mean of X scores.
$r_{XY} =$ correlation between X and Y scores.

making the transformation:

$$x = \frac{X - \overline{X}}{S_X}$$

$$y = \frac{Y - \overline{Y}}{S_Y},$$

where x and y are true standard variables with unit sigmas and zero means, we may write equation (1) as:

$$x = ry \qquad \cdots \qquad \cdots \qquad \cdots \qquad \cdots \qquad \cdots \qquad (2)$$

As we are here dealing with normalized standard scores on both variables, equation (2) was graphed by the substitution of three arbitrarily chosen values for y (in S.M.), together with $r = 0·81014$.

Thus, when

$y = -1·0$ S.M. (40 S.S.); $x = -0·81$ S.M. (41·9 S.S.).
$y = 0·0$ S.M. (50 S.S.); $x = 0·00$ S.M. (50·0 S.S.).
$y = +1·0$ S.M. (60 S.S.); $x = +0·81$ S.M. (58·1 S.S.).

In a similar manner the 1% and 5% upper confidence lines were graphed by means of the following equation:

$$X = \frac{rS_X}{S_Y}(Y - \overline{Y}) + \overline{X} + t_p S_X \sqrt{1 - r^2} \qquad \cdots \qquad \cdots \qquad (3)$$

Hence:

$$\frac{Y - \overline{Y}}{S_Y} = \frac{1}{r}\left[\frac{X - \overline{X}}{S_X} - t_p\sqrt{1 - r^2}\right] \qquad \cdots \qquad \cdots \qquad (4)$$

which in the case of true standard variables with unit sigmas and zero means can be reduced to the form:

$$y = \frac{1}{r}\left(x - t_p\sqrt{1 - r^2}\right) \qquad \cdots \qquad \cdots \qquad \cdots \qquad (5)$$

Equation (5) was plotted equating t_p to 2·32635, and 1·64487 in the case of the 1% and 5% upper confidence lines respectively.

ANNEXURE A

TESTING PROGRAMME — ADMINISTRATIVE TRAINEES

I. FIRST DAY'S PROCEEDINGS

	TESTS	TIME ALLOWED	ACTUAL TIMES	REMARKS
1	Introductory Address	30	08.30 — 09.00	
2	Biographical Data Sheet	50	09.00 — 09.50	
3	Test A(F)	35 + 5	09.50 — 10.30	
	Tea interval	15	10.30 — 10.45	
4	Projection Tests—Incomplete Sentences .	30 + 5	10.45 — 11.20	
	Self-description .	15 + 5	11.20 — 11.40	
5	Test M	20 + 5	11.40 — 12.05	
6	Test H	30 + 5	12.05 — 12.40	
	Lunch interval	80	12.40 — 2.00	
7	Test G	20 + 5	2.00 — 2.25	
8	General Knowledge Test	30 + 5	2.25 — 3.00	
9	Group Discussion	60	3.00 — 4.00	
10	Allocation of Assignment—Project 1 .	30	4.00 — 4.30	

II. SECOND DAY'S PROCEEDINGS

Group I (1-8)

Times	Project Interview Tester 1	Project Interview Tester 2	Clinical Interview R.O. 1	Project 1 Report Tester 3
A.M.				
08.30—09.30	1	2	3, 4	5, 6, 7, 8
09.30—10.30	3	4	1, 2	1, 2, 3, 4
10.45—11.45	5	6	7, 8	
11.45—12.45	7	8	5, 6	
P.M.				
2.00—5.30	Assigned Leadership Test (Committee) (Each candidate 25 minutes) (R.O. 1 plus additional Assessors)			
5.30—6.00	Sociometric Questionnaire			

Group II (9-16)

Times	Project Interview Tester 1	Project Interview Tester 2	Clinical Interview R.O. 2	Project 1 Report Tester 3
A.M.				
08.30—12.00	Assigned Leadership Test (Committee) (Each candidate 25 minutes) (R.O. 2 plus additional Assessors)			
P.M.				
1.30—2.30	9	10	11, 12	13, 14, 15, 16
2.30—3.30	11	12	9, 10	9, 10, 11, 12
3.30—4.30	13	14	15, 16	
4.30—5.30	15	16	13, 14	
5.30—6.00	Sociometric Questionnaire			

RATING SCALE USED FOR CRITERION 4

Confidential

Employee's surname:...

Christian names:..

Check No.:..

Section in which employed:...

Period of service in Section: From.................................. To..................................

....

Name of Assessor:..

Position held by Assessor:..

How long has Assessor had personal acquaintance with employee's work?

From.. To..

Please rate the above employee on each of the qualities listed below, *and record your comments in the space provided.*

N.B. 1. Rate employees by placing the appropriate number in the square provided, where

1 = inferior	4 = high average
2 = below average	5 = above average
3 = low average	6 = superior

2. No rating will be counted unless it is accompanied by supporting comments.

3. Where the Assessor genuinely feels he is not in a position to pass judgement, the section should be left blank.

In order to assist Assessors a guide has been provided, which defines the qualities which should be considered under each heading.

I. Mental Abilities — General

(1) Intelligence. *Rating:*

(2) Reasoning ability. *Rating:*

II. Mental Abilities — Special

(1) Bilingual ability. *Rating:*

(2) Ability in the use of language. *Rating:*

(3) Ability in the use of numbers or figures. *Rating:*

(4) Organizing ability. *Rating:*

(5) Ability to deal with people. *Rating:*

III. Personality

(1) Drive and effort. *Rating:*

(2) Self-confidence. *Rating:*

(3) Dependability. *Rating:*

(4) Personal maturity. *Rating:*

(5) Motivation. *Rating:*

IV. General Comments

GUIDE TO THE COMPLETION OF SUPERVISOR'S REPORT ON ADMINISTRATIVE TRAINEES

Criterion 4

When completing the report form on employees working or being trained in your section, you should familiarize yourself thoroughly with the definitions and examples given below, before recording your comments.

The object of this guide is to focus attention on to the important qualities, and also to introduce uniformity in all supervisors' reports, so that these may be put on a comparable basis for the overall assessment of employees.

You should not withhold an honest opinion. Wherever possible support your comments by quoting examples and mentioning incidents.

Section I (1): Intelligence

Here you should think of the candidate's ability to grasp quickly what is required of him in a given situation. Questions which you should ask yourself are:

Is he quick on the uptake?

Does he cotton-on to things easily?

Does he comprehend instructions quickly and easily, or does he require a repetition of these before catching on?

Does he in fact carry out the instructions properly, as given, or is the end result hopelessly at variance with the instructions?

Section I (2): Reasoning Ability

Here you should think of the candidate's ability to think his way clearly through a problem. Questions to ask yourself are:

Is he systematic in his approach?

Does he grasp the essential features of the problem, or is his thinking cluttered up by irrelevant and non-essential detail?

Is his working-out of the problem logical, or are there inconsistencies and *non sequiturs* in his thinking?

Does he marshal facts in support of his conclusions effectively and concisely, or are his arguments woolly and vague?

Section II (1): Bilingual Ability

Here you should report on the facility with which the candidate uses both, in speech and in writing, the *other tongue* (as opposed to *his mother tongue*).

Consider the varying degrees of proficiency:

(i) Can understand when spoken to.

(ii) Can understand and can make himself understood in simple terms only (e.g. as when talking to bus conductors, or asking his way, etc.).

(iii) Has sufficient knowledge of the *other tongue* to be able to hold a casual conversation or draft a routine business letter without grammatical mistakes.

(iv) Has sufficient knowledge of the *other tongue* to be able to deliver a lecture, make a speech, or write an essay on non-technical subjects.

(v) Is more proficient in the *other tongue* than 90% of people having this as their *mother tongue*.

Section II (2): Ability in the Use of Language

Here you should report on the facility with which the candidate can express himself (both in speech and in writing) through the medium of the language in which he is most proficient. Does he, for example, express his ideas clearly, fluently, and concisely? Consider also the economy of effort with which he gets his ideas across. Is he clumsy? Does he hunt for words? Is he vague and woolly? Does he go in for a lot of circumlocution?

Section II (3): Ability in the Use of Numbers or Figures

Here you should report on the ability with which the candidate manipulates and comprehends data in numerical form:

Is he quick and accurate when working with figures?

Does he find it easy to think in terms of numerical data?

Section II (4): Organizing Ability

Here you should comment on the candidate's ability to plan procedures and also to see these through to the desired end.

For example:

> Is the plan straightforward and at the same time effective, rather than complicated and cumbersome?
>
> Does he show imagination in allowing for special contingencies or outside interferences?
>
> Does he tend to fuss even when things are going all right?
>
> Does he get flustered when unforeseen difficulties arise, or is he capable of effective improvisation?
>
> Does the plan work easily and smoothly?

Section II (5): Ability to Deal with People

Here one should comment on the candidate's ability to get on with, and work effectively in collaboration with, other members of staff both senior and junior, and other trainees.

For example:

> Can he work with others without friction or misunderstanding developing?
>
> When he encounters hostility or resentment from others, does he cope successfully with the situation?
>
> Can he stand up for himself without becoming too aggressive and destroying thereby good relations?
>
> Does he submit to opposition or hostility too easily, thereby reducing his effectiveness as a worker?
>
> Does he usually manage to win the co-operation of others?
>
> Does he use tact in dealing with people, or does he tend to be blunt and offhand in his relations?

Section III (1): Drive and Effort

Here one should comment on the candidate's ability to maintain effort in the accomplishment of a particular task.

For example:

> Does he put his back into the work?
>
> Does he keep going, or does he tend to quit half-way?
>
> Is he a prompt starter or is he slow in getting off the mark?
>
> Does he finish off his work neatly, or does he tend to leave loose ends lying about?
>
> Does he take on new work readily, or does he tend to find excuses for not doing things?
>
> Does he tend to 'palm' his work off on to others?
>
> Does he tend to visit with others, talk and waste time instead of getting down to work?

Section III (2): Self-Confidence

Here one should assess the candidate's behaviour in terms of such questions as:

Does he get on with his work or assignment without asking for assistance, or is he dependent on others for this?

Is he diffident about undertaking a job, or does he accept the responsibility readily?

Does he find it impossible to proceed with his work without asking innumerable footling questions?

Is he reluctant to ask others for assistance when it is necessary and consequently just goes blundering along?

Is he capable of making his own decisions?

Must he be shown every step in the procedure?

Is he constantly seeking confirmation or approval by asking such questions as 'Am I right?' or 'How am I doing?'

Does he resent criticism?

Is he easily angered, and does he tend to 'fly off the handle'?

Does he on occasions express self-doubts concerning his ability to cope with tasks?

Section III (3): Dependability

Here one should comment on the extent to which a candidate can be relied upon to carry out a given assignment.

For example:

Can one depend on the accuracy of his work, or does one always have to check it to make sure he has not overlooked important issues, or made mistakes?

Can one depend on his word when he tells you that something has been done, or gives you some information?

When he tells you that he will see to something, can you forget about it knowing that it will be attended to satisfactorily?

Is he thorough in whatever he undertakes?

Section III (4): Personal Maturity

Here one should comment on the extent to which the candidate's behaviour is free from childish mannerisms. One should also mention his degree of self-control.

For example:

Has he any traits which are excessive and dominate his personality?

Is he co-operative when working with others?

Is he easy and pleasant to get on with?

Has he any tendency to sulk?

Does he display childish attitudes towards anything?

Is he childish in his behaviour?

Is he considerate or selfish in his dealings with others?

Is he excessively pleasing and ingratiating in his manner?

Is he subject to fads or whims?

Can he take an impersonal and objective view of a situation or does he allow personal prejudices to obtrude themselves?

SECTION III (5): MOTIVATION

Here one should comment on the extent to which the candidate shows himself to be really keen to get on in his work.

For example:

Is he quite willing to undertake tasks assigned to him even though they may be of a routine and menial nature?

Does he show himself ready to learn?

Does he make efforts to improve his performance?

Is he amenable to instruction?

Does he tend to carry on working after hours, or does he 'down tools' on the stroke of the clock?

Is he the type who normally gives that 'little bit extra' over and above what is required?

SECTION IV: GENERAL COMMENTS

In this section you should make a note of any feature of the candidate's behaviour, performance, or personality make-up, which has not been referred to in the above sections.

10

ANNEXURE C

GRADING SCALE USED FOR CRITERION 5

In this situation you are asked to assign the employee to a particular grade on the scale of potentiality for administrative work. In doing so you should consider the height of the individual's occupational ceiling in the universe of clerical and administrative jobs.

In deciding upon a given level you should consider how far the individual could climb up this scale were he given sufficient opportunity, encouragement and training. In other words, given all the opportunities, what is the highest point at which the individual could function efficiently, and cope completely with the job's requirements?

When considering the scale one should not be upset by preconceived meanings of the words *clerical, executive,* and *administrative.* Their use here is purely for convenience, and one should rather think in terms of the definitions given for the specific purpose of this Supervisor's Report Form.

C-Class or clerical jobs refer to work of a purely routine clerical nature and involve the fairly straightforward carrying-out of set procedures in the manipulation of numerical or verbal data. The incumbent is not required to show initiative in developing new methods, but is mainly responsible to others for accurate and reliable work.

B-Class or executive jobs refer to positions in which the incumbent is given certain freedom in the execution of plans or policies which have been laid down by higher authority. There is scope in these positions for individual initiative and imagination, planning and organizing ability. The responsibilities carried by these posts are fairly heavy for they are the organizers who bring together men, materials and machines in a manner which actually gets the work done.

A-Class or administrative jobs refer to positions which are concerned with the formulation of policies or drawing up of plans. The incumbents are expected to possess knowledge, experience, and wisdom; and to be able to make shrewd assessments of the values and potentialities of men, machines and systems. The responsibilities of these positions are heavy, for on them rests in the first instance the success of the industrial undertaking as a whole, by planning the effective co-ordination of constituent elements, and being able to think into the future.

Indicate the employee's potentiality for development in administrative and clerical work, by placing a (X) in the appropriate square below:

A+	A	A−	B+	B	B−	C+	C	C−
Senior Administrator	Administrator	Junior Administrator	Senior Executive	Executive	Junior Executive	Senior Clerical	Clerical	Junior Clerical

....
Signature

149

ANNEXURE D

THEORETICAL SELECTION OF ADMINISTRATIVE TRAINEES FOR CRITERION 6

In this task you are asked to assume that *no other* candidates are available for the above Trainee Scheme, and that a certain number *have* to be selected from the attached list.

We would like you to indicate which candidates you consider to possess the *most potentiality*, and *least potentiality*, for training and development in the field of administrative work, by carrying out the following procedures:

(*a*) From the list of candidates select the *one* whom you consider to be the *best suited*. Remove his name from the list and record it opposite the figure 1 below.

From those names that are left in the list again select the *best suited*, remove his name from the list, and record it opposite figure 2.

In the case of this particular list we should like you to repeat this procedure .... times.

(1) ....

(2) ....

(3) ....

(4) ....

(*b*) From the names that are left in the list after procedure (*a*) has been carried out, we ask you to select the *least suited*; remove his name from the list and record it opposite figure 1 below.

Again in this particular case we should like you to repeat this procedure .... times.

(1) ....

(2) ....

(3) ....

(4) ....

Signature :...

N.B. Please attach the original list of candidates to this form when completed.

ANNEXURE E

COUNCIL FOR SCIENTIFIC AND INDUSTRIAL RESEARCH

NATIONAL INSTITUTE FOR PERSONNEL RESEARCH

TRIAL INTERVIEW

Confidential

This test is not to be shown to unauthorized
persons, or used without the permission of the
National Institute for Personnel Research.

*Do not make notes on or mark in any way the pages
of this test, as it has to be used again by others.*

[Time allowed: 1 hour]

Project No. 2: Trial Interview

INSTRUCTIONS TO INTERVIEWER

Time allowed: one hour

You are required to imagine that you hold the position of Chief Works
Accountant at the Pretoria Works of the S.A. Industrial Corporation.

Since the war your work has increased considerably due to a general
development of the industry; so much so that the General Manager
approved of your recommendation to create a new post of Private
Secretary (female) to assist you. There was, unfortunately, no female
employee in your department senior enough, or possessing the desirable
qualifications to a sufficient degree, to enable you to promote a junior
member of your staff to this post. Thus your only way of filling the post
was by means of advertisement in the local papers.

Assignment

You will find attached hereto copies of the following:

(1) A copy of the advertisement which appeared in the press.

(2) A Job Analysis indicating in precise detail exactly what is
required of the incumbent in this post.

(3) A letter of application from a Miss P. C. van Jaarsveld together
with supporting testimonials.

You will be allowed *one hour* in which to interview Miss van Jaarsveld
and write a report on your findings. This report should contain:

(a) Your decision as to whether you consider Miss van Jaarsveld a suitable candidate for this post; and, if so, what commencing salary you would offer her.

(b) A full statement giving the reasons for your decision in (a).

When you are satisfied that you understand the implications of this assignment, call for Miss van Jaarsveld and commence your interview.

Do not write any notes on, or mark in any way, the pages of this assignment, for it has to be used again.

[Copy of the advertisement appearing in the local papers for the position of Private Secretary (Female) to the Chief Accountant.]

SOUTH AFRICAN INDUSTRIAL CORPORATION

VACANCY: PRIVATE SECRETARY

Applications are invited from suitably qualified persons for the post of Private Secretary (Female) to the Chief Accountant of the S.A. Industrial Corporation.

The post carries with it attractive service conditions and excellent opportunities for promotion.

The successful candidate will be expected to be highly proficient in shorthand and typing (both English and Afrikaans) and, in addition, to have had some training and/or experience in bookkeeping, or accounting work. Previous experience as a Private Secretary is not essential, but a practical knowledge of general office routine and filing methods will be a necessary recommendation.

Salary scale: £360 x 30 — £420 (efficiency barrier) x 30 — £480 plus a cost-of-living allowance of £50 p.a.

The commencing salary will be determined according to the successful candidate's qualifications and experience.

Membership of the Corporation's Provident and Sick Benefit Funds will be compulsory.

Applications stating age, qualifications, and experience, and the earliest date on which duties can be assumed, must reach the Secretary, S.A. Industrial Corporation, P.O. Box 196, Johannesburg, not later than 15th November, 1948.

JOB ANALYSIS: PRIVATE SECRETARY (FEMALE)*

(i) *Nature of Job*

1. To open all correspondence addressed to the chief accountant (except that marked private or personal).

---

* The author is indebted to The Industrial Welfare Society, Robert Hyde House, 48 Bryanston Square, London, W. 1, for permission to quote, with amendments, this job analysis from the work of Rice, A. K. (1947), *Assessing the Job*, Industrial Welfare Society Monograph, Second Edition. Minor alterations were made in the original job analysis to fit into the context of the test and local conditions.

2. To take down and reproduce replies, as dictated by the chief accountant.

3. To draft replies to routine letters for the chief accountant's signature.

4. To arrange appointments on behalf of the chief accountant and those who wish to see him.

5. To distribute papers from the chief accountant's office, as directed.

6. To keep private filing.

7. To remind the chief accountant of meetings, conferences and other matters which need his attention.

8. To answer the telephone and keep inquirers posted of the where-abouts of the chief accountant.

9. To receive visitors to the chief accountant and to handle appropriately those whom the chief accountant does not want to see.

10. Generally to organize the chief accountant's own office, so that he does not spend unnecessary time on routine.

(ii) *Personal Relationships Involved*

The private secretary to the chief accountant is responsible to the chief accountant only, who is the head of the department. This is the only private secretary's job within the accounts department, but there are ten other jobs of private secretarial status within the organization. Primarily, the private secretary has a close personal relationship with the chief accountant, but she will perhaps do some work, as directed by the chief accountant, for his chief assistants, and she will therefore have close relations with them and to a lesser extent with the chief clerks in charge of the various sections. She will have regular contact with all senior members of the accounts and other departments' staff, on behalf of the chief accountant.

All visitors to the chief accountant will normally pass through her office and she will have normal personal relations with other clerical staff in the higher grades.

(iii) *Conditions of Service*

   (a) *Salary.* Grade 4. Clerical Staff. Range for age 23 and over £360 x £30 — £420 (efficiency barrier) x £30 — £480 plus c.o.l.a. Paid monthly by cheque on last Friday of calendar month.

   (b) *Hours of work.* Normal office hours are 9 a.m. to 5 p.m.; five days per week; extra hours may be required when the chief accountant is busy; no overtime payment is made for this.

   (c) *Holidays.* All statutory holidays and two weeks' annual holiday.

   (d) *Pension.* Contributory staff pension scheme as published in the company's booklet.

   (e) *Notice.* The job is permanent and one month's notice is given and required on termination.

(*f*) *Possible promotion.* It is possible that the private secretary could transfer to the typing staff as supervisor.

(iv) *Demands*

1. *Physical.* There are no special physical demands and physical conditions are considered very comfortable. Sex: female; age limits 25–45 years.

2. *Technical and educational.* General education of secondary standard to J.C. or over. Technical education in shorthand, typing and general office routine. Speeds desirable are shorthand, 120 words per minute; typing, 65 words per minute.

3. *Practical experience.* Previous experience as a private secretary is not essential, but practical experience of filing and shorthand and typing is essential. Experience in book-keeping methods.

4. *General and personal.* The private secretary is in a position which makes considerable personal demands and at the same time is capable of giving considerable satisfaction. It is essential that she should like working for the chief accountant as a person rather than as an employer. Her work is officially that of a senior clerical worker in the organization, but it must develop a very personal character and, inevitably, service of a quite private nature will be asked of her.

The pressure of work is governed almost entirely by the pressure on the chief accountant; she has little chance, therefore, to plan an orderly day's work. She will be constantly interrupted when she is doing letters, etc., by a buzzer summoning her to the chief accountant or by people who wish to see the chief accountant. Such interruptions and alterations of plans have to be accepted pleasantly and willingly, and must not cause confusion to the work.

Her behaviour to visitors and telephone inquirers will have a considerable effect on their relations with the chief accountant. It is important, therefore, that she recognizes her position as the chief accountant's first contact with other employees of the organization and with visitors from outside.

Her status with her fellow workers is enhanced by her knowing confidential information, but resistance to attempts at getting information may be resented and conceivably alienate her from her colleagues. Her standing in the organization depends to a considerable extent on the standing of the chief accountant.

Summary

It is a job which demands considerable personal loyalty to one man, with all the demands it can make and the satisfaction it can give. The work varies from very dull routine to the position of having almost to deputize for the chief accountant in his personal contacts. It demands a liking for meeting people, good shorthand and typing, but above all the wish and desire to work in close relationship with the chief accountant.

LETTER OF APPLICATION

128 Arcadia Mansions,
Kirkness Street,
PRETORIA.
10th November, 1948.
Phone 2-8611.

The Secretary,
S.A. Industrial Corporation Ltd.,
P.O. Box 196,
JOHANNESBURG.

Dear Sir,

VACANCY: PRIVATE SECRETARY (FEMALE)

With reference to your advertisement appearing in the *Pretoria News* on 1st November, 1948, I hereby wish to apply for the post of Private Secretary (Female) to the Chief Accountant.

In support of my application I submit herewith the following information regarding my qualifications and experience:

Age: 27 years. *Date of birth:* 12th June, 1921 (Durban).

Education:

(a) Primary School for Girls (Durban) 1927–35.

(b) Girls' High School (Pietermaritzburg) 1936–40.

Certificates held:

(a) Matriculation Certificate (2nd Class), 1940.

(b) Intermediate National Commercial Certificate, 1941.
Shorthand, 100 w.p.m. Typing, 60 w.p.m.

(c) Intermediate National Commercial Certificate in Bookkeeping, 1941.

Experience:

In 1942 my father was transferred to Pretoria and since that time I have had wide experience of clerical and secretarial work in both the Public Service and private organizations. In the various posts which I have held, my work has involved a considerable amount of shorthand and typing, the handling, filing and despatch of correspondence, and routine office administration.

Owing to the fact that for the last year I have held a more senior post, my speed in shorthand and typing has suffered somewhat, but I feel confident that with some further training I shall regain my ability in this connection.

Unfortunately I am unable to furnish three testimonials as requested in your advertisement, as the Public Service does not give personal references. I am, however, enclosing two testimonials from private organizations in which I was previously employed, together with a certificate of character from the Ds. S. R. van Broekhuizen.

As I am not in employment at present, I am in a position to assume duty as soon as requested.

Trusting my application will receive your favourable consideration,

I am, Sir,

Your obedient servant,

P. C. van Jaarsveld (Miss).

THE SCOTTBURGH PRIVATE HOSPITAL

Tel. Address: 'Hospital'   P.O. Box 315,
Phone: 187 Scottburgh   SCOTTBURGH.
                                             20 March 1947.

To Whom It May Concern

This is to certify that P. C. VAN JAARSVELD was employed at this Hospital in the capacity of Assistant Secretary and Almoner, from 1st January, 1946, to 31st March, 1947.

Miss van Jaarsveld's duties involved the admission of patients, rendering of accounts and the maintenance of hospital fee books and case records.

I can state with pleasure that Miss van Jaarsveld's work was always faithfully carried out, and of a high order. Her pleasant and obliging manner assisted in no small measure in maintaining the friendly and co-operative atmosphere in which the work of our staff was carried out.

Miss van Jaarsveld leaves us to improve her own position, and I have no hesitation in recommending her for her new post of responsibility and trust.

(*sgd.*) P. SMITH
Secretary.

THE 'ALIBABA' MOTOR ENGINEERING COY. LTD.

Directors: JABULA HOUSE,   Telegrams and Cables:
S. FISH   SALMON ROAD,   'ALIBABA'
T. COETZEE   SCOTTBURGH   Phone: Scottburgh 137
L. MANN   *Our reference:*
P. V. D. MERWE   4824/S.   HH/P.v.d.M.

11th July, 1948.

To Whom It May Concern:

This is to certify that

PETRONELLA CORNELIA VAN JAARSVELD

has been in our employment for the period 1 April '47 to 31 July '48, during which time she held the position of Secretary/Bookkeeper.

Miss van Jaarsveld was responsible for handling all correspondence, and had full charge of the company's books. She thus held a position of trust and responsibility in this Company.

We have no hesitation in stating that Miss van Jaarsveld's work was always efficiently carried out, and the accuracy of her book-keeping received favourable comment from our external auditors.

Miss van Jaarsveld leaves us of her own free will with our best wishes for her future success. We can recommend her with confidence to anyone seeking a pleasant, trustworthy, and capable worker.

(*Sgd.*) P. v. d. MERWE

Director.

„Gerus",

Penzanceweg 120,

DURBAN.

1 Feb. 1942.

H. D. L.

Hiermee word verklaar dat ek PETRONELLA CORNELIA VAN JAARSVELD ken vanaf haar kinderjare, en kan daarvoor instaan dat sy in 'n Christelike omgewing grootgeword het, en gebaat het van die voordele van 'n eerlike en opregte opvoeding.

Petronella het 'n baie aangename geaardheid; sy is vriendelik, hulpsaam, opreg, en is netjies in haar voorkoms. Sy het aktief deel geneem in funksies wat van tyd tot tyd vir liefdadigheid gehou is, en het met besondere bekwaamheid en bereidwilligheid aan die verrigtinge meegedoen. Sy het ook op die komitee van die Strewersvereniging gedien.

Op skool het Petronella haar studies met nougesette aandag aangepak, en het die eindeksamen met 'n tweede klas geslaag. Sy het aktief deelgeneem aan sport en het daar ook haar besondere karaktertrek van leierskap aan die dag gelê.

Dis met graagte dat ek Petronella aanbeveel vir 'n vakante betrekking vir 'n eerlike en vertroubare dame.

(*geteken*) Ds. S. R. VAN BROEKHUIZEN.

INSTRUCTIONS TO INTERVIEWEE

You are to imagine that you are a Miss PETRONELLA CORNELIA VAN JAARSVELD who has applied for the post of Private Secretary (Female) to the Chief Accountant of the S.A. Industrial Corporation.

The advertisement appeared in the *Pretoria News* on 1 November 1948. You have already submitted your application with supporting testimonials (see Assignment to Interviewer), and have now been called for interview by the Chief Accountant.

The following are the facts of your biographical record:

Age: 27. *Date of birth:* 12 June 1921 (Durban).

Family domicile since birth: Durban, 1921–42; Pretoria, 1942–

Father's age: 54.

Mother's age: 50.

Siblings: 1 B — 30.

         1 S — 29

Father's occupation: Branch manager of Phillips Shoe Coy.
                      Transferred to Pretoria Branch 1942.

Education:

(*a*) Primary School for Girls (Durban): 1927–35.

Age .	6	7	8	9	10	11	12	13	14
Year .	27	28	29	30	31	32	33	34	35
Std. .	aI	aII	I	II	III	IV	V	VI	VI

(Failed Std. VI in 1934)

The real reason for your failure in Std. VI, 1934, was 'laziness' and a disinclination to be bothered with school work—not because of lack of ability. You will naturally attempt to conceal this fact in interview by finding some plausible excuse, e.g. you think the Durban climate had a lot to do with it.

(*b*) Secondary School

Age . . .	15	16	17	18	19
Year . . .	36	37	38	39	40
Std. . . .	VII	VIII	VIII	IX	X

(Failed J.C. in 1938. Matric. 2nd Class 1940.)

You attribute your failure in J.C. to the fact that you have always 'loathed Arithmetic' and on top of that you had a horrible Maths. teacher, who always 'had it in for you'. You thus failed Arithmetic and consequently the whole examination.

The real reason was the fact that at the beginning of 1938 you had persuaded your father to take you away from the boarding establishment and allow you to live out with your aunt. In these circumstances you had found time for, for example, dancing, picnics, etc. The aunt was a very kind and understanding one whom you could easily get round.

(*c*) *Commercial*

In 1941 you attended full-time the Technical College, Durban, and gained the following certificates:

(1) Intermediate National Commercial Certificate in Shorthand and Typewriting (Bilingual): 100 and 60 words per minute respectively.

(2) National Commercial Certificate in Bookkeeping (Intermediate).

You were then under your parents' watchful eye and were compelled to study diligently, although you found no real difficulty in taking these courses full-time in a year, with plenty of time to spare for parties.

Occupational record

Your father was transferred on promotion to the Pretoria Branch of the firm and you went with your family to take up your first appointment as a typist/clerk in the Public Service.

Dept. or firm	Job	Time	Nature of duties
1. Department of Revenue.	Typist/Clerk £15 p.m.	Jan. '42 Feb. '43	Assistant to the Staff Clerk handling and posting personal records of junior members of staff. Typing of correspondence.
2. Department of Census and Statistics.	Senior Shorthand Typist £15 p.m.	Mar. '43 to June '44	Shorthand Typist in Administrative Office of the Director. Typing of reports, memoranda, assisting Senior Clerk (male) in administration.
3. Senior School for Girls (Pretoria).	Secretary to Headmistress £18 10s. p.m.	July '44 to Dec. '45	Bookkeeping, the handling of accounts, filing and dispatch of correspondence, typing of examination stencils, ordering of stocks and supplies, etc.

Resigned from Public Service December 1945.

Dept. or firm	Job	Time	Nature of duties
4. Scottburgh Private Hospital (see testimonial).	Asst. Sec. and Almoner £24 10s. p.m.	Jan. '46 to Mar. '47	Admission of patients, rendering of accounts, maintenance of hospital fee books and case records—Admin. staff. Controller of three.
5. 'Alibaba' Motor Engineering Coy., Scottburgh (see testimonial).	Secretary/ Bookkeeper £29 p.m.	Apr. '47 to July '48	In full charge of company's books and correspondence. Controller junior staff: one typist and one clerk.

From the above record it will be apparent that your occupational history has been a varied one and one which should equip you admirably for the post for which you have applied. It will thus be your aim in the interview to exploit this fact whenever opportunity presents itself.

However, there is one great weakness in your record which would be a disqualifying factor and which you must be at great pains to conceal— viz. that your record has been a shiftless one. To the casual observer this is not apparent, for there may be good reasons to explain all your occupational changes. They may have been innocent transfers in the Public

Service arising out of circumstances over which you had no control; and later on they may be interpreted as advancement. However, in your case the explanation is to be found in the fact that you are the type who is shiftless, not prepared to put up with personal inconvenience, not prepared to give anything a 'real go', and has no compunction about walking out. You become easily upset and dissatisfied and are constantly wanting 'change' of environment. Your philosophy is 'suck the world, or you are had for a sucker'. Your outstanding ability has enabled you always to get away with these personality and temperament defects. Your habit of mind is of long standing for it affected also your school record. This description of your personality is substantiated by the real reasons for the changes in your occupational history: viz. these reveal the fact that all changes have been initiated by you yourself and had come about as requests for transfer, and resignations for personal reasons.

(1) You found the work boring and monotonous.

(2) The Chief Clerk was always picking on you and bullying you in the work.

(3) You felt there was no future in the Civil Service—and that you could get a higher salary outside. In any case you wanted a change—to get away from Pretoria and from the family's apron-strings—to be on your own and lead your own life. To go to the coast.

(4) You got sick of seeing the 'sick and lame and lazy'. You wanted to get away from the hospital atmosphere. In any case the Alibaba Coy. offered you a nice rise in salary.

(5) You had an unpleasant personal experience at Scottburgh (you were 'taken for a ride' by one of the directors) and wanted to get back to your people in Pretoria. (For the first time you had not had things all your own way.)

Comments

During the interview no information must be volunteered or 'put on a plate' for the interviewer. You should make the most of your good points and qualifications, and exploit the advantages of your varied experience. Your personality defect should only be suggested in the first place by a certain reluctance on your part to discuss 'reasons for changes'. In the case of the Public Service your first answer can be 'I was transferred', and in the latter cases you can give 'personal reasons' as your reason. Only if the interviewer is not to be put off in this connection, and pursues the matter, should you state the reasons in the form given above.

COUNCIL FOR SCIENTIFIC AND INDUSTRIAL RESEARCH
NATIONAL INSTITUTE FOR PERSONNEL RESEARCH

SHELTERED EMPLOYMENT STORY

Confidential

This Test is not to be shown to unauthorized
persons, or used without the permission of
the National Institute for Personnel Research

PROJECT NO. 1: SHELTERED EMPLOYMENT STORY

Time allowed: One hour

I. INTRODUCTION

As a result of the last war a national organization was created by certain
influential and public-spirited individuals who felt that a more useful and
meaningful form of memorial should be erected in honour of all those who
had fallen. The idea caught the imagination of the people, who contributed generously by way of street collections, individual grants and
endowments from private organizations (regimental associations, etc.).
It also elicited the support of the Government in the form of an annual
subsidy.

This organization, known as the *National War Memorial Foundation*,
decided that it would create a memorial in the form of an Ex-servicemen's
Sheltered Employment Farm and Community Centre, where married
disabled ex-volunteers could live a useful and full life until such time as
they were successfully rehabilitated, and could take part in normal employment and the activities of the outside community.

II. PROJECT

You are required to imagine that you have just been appointed as
manager of this Sheltered Employment Farm and Community Centre.

In taking up the appointment the Foundation's Council has naturally
acquainted you with its general policy and supplied you with all information available, to enable you to get a general picture of the scheme and
make the necessary recommendations for its implementation.

III. GENERAL POLICY OF THE COUNCIL

(a) The scheme is intended to provide sheltered employment and a community centre for thirty disabled ex-volunteers and their families.

(b) The sheltered employment is intended to be of two main types:

(i) An industrial or quasi-industrial (e.g. leather-work, weaving, etc.).

(ii) Agricultural (crop-growing, market gardening, flower gardening, etc.).

At the same time the project is intended to cater for the social life of the Community Centre; to enable the families who cannot afford the amenities of the outside world to live a full and happy life.

(c) It is not intended that the ex-volunteer and his family shall be permanent residents, living an isolated and sheltered existence for the rest of their lives. It is intended that during their sojourn they shall undergo treatment and learn some new occupation which will enable them to be fitted in again into the normal life of the outside community. It is thus expected that the population will be a gradually shifting one and that many ex-volunteers will, in the course of time, benefit from the facilities provided.

(d) Later on, after perhaps five or eight years, when no more suitable ex-volunteers are in need of rehabilitation, the ex-volunteer qualification for admission will be withdrawn and the facilities made available to the 'casualties' of everyday life.

In this way the memory of the fallen will be preserved in an institution which is ever bringing help to the 'wounded' and assisting them back into the security of normal life.

IV. GENERAL INFORMATION

(a) Description of Farm

The farm consists of some 400 acres of land situated mostly east of the Buffelsburg range of hills. It is watered, apart from rain, by two streams, an eastern and a western, on which have already been constructed two dams in a fairly crude fashion. The western stream, during the dry season, runs at an average depth of 2 ft., the eastern at an average depth of $1\frac{1}{2}$ ft. The maximum and minimum widths of the two streams at this time of the year are: western 3 ft. and 2 ft.; eastern 2 ft. and $1\frac{1}{2}$ ft. respectively.

The *soil* of the farm is apt to be clayey, and, though well supplied with organic matter, is principally lacking in phosphates. Between the two streams the topsoil is, on an average, 8 ft. deep. A dolomite outcrop (see map) is found on the eastern ridge. The western slopes are somewhat shaley, and for that reason are not suitable for cultivation.

Approximately one-half of the farm lying between the streams can, if necessary, be irrigated, and is good agricultural ground. The rest, except for a small portion in the west, and for the higher reaches of the two large hills, is good grazing ground.

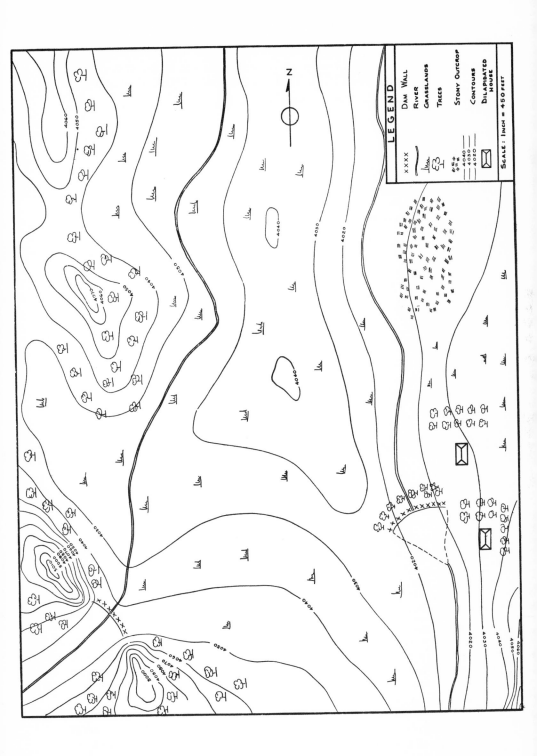

LEGEND

DAM WALL	xxxx
RIVER	
GRASSLANDS	
TREES	
STONY OUTCROP	
CONTOURS	4040 4030 4020
DILAPIDATED HOUSE	

SCALE : 1 INCH = 450 FEET

The land has been profitably farmed in the past by two market-gardeners (Portuguese) who confined their activities to the irrigated land on the western banks of the eastern stream.

Sheep, cattle and horses do well on the neighbouring farms and could, if necessary, be farmed here. Dipping is essential to check the spread of tickborne diseases.

Maize, vegetables, soya beans, berries and other fruit (not tropical) flourish.

The natural grasses consist of rooigras with certain types of clover. The grass in the grasslands is slightly sour, and is thus good for grazing in summer, and haymaking in early spring and summer. Winter feed is scarce. The hills are covered by a species of acacia-tree with grass between them.

An analysis of the soil in the lower portion of the farm was made by a Government expert. The table follows:

Chemical composition	Soil %	Subsoil %
Hygroscopic moisture . .	14·75	14·22
Organic and volatile matter (incl. nitrogen) . . .	13·64	11·53
Insoluble matter . . .	44·52	45·86
Iron oxide and alumina .	26·30	27·97
Lime	0·10	0·03
Magnesia	0·30	0·26
Potash	0·15	0·21
Soda	0·09	0·07
Phosphoric oxide . . .	0·10	0·07
Sulphur Trioxide . . .	0·06	0·05
Chlorine	0·002	—
Carbon dioxide	0·003	0·006
Mechanical composition		
Moisture	14·9	14·2
Organic and volatile matter	13·6	11·5
Fine gravel	2·2	3·0
Coarse sand	1·2	1·1
Fine sand	19·1	16·0
Silt	12·2	14·7
Fine silt	18·4	11·4
Clay	18·4	28·3

There are no fences, roads or buildings on the farm apart from the two dilapidated houses (one three-roomed and one four-roomed).

These houses will, however, not lend themselves to renovation for European habitation.

The average height of the farm is 4,040 ft. with the two highest peaks, Scylla and Charybdis, 5,000 ft. and 5,010 ft. respectively, situated to the south-west.

The *climate* is in general mild, though heavy frosts fall during the winter months. The following is a chart of the average temperatures for the last ten years.

Month	Maximum	Minimum	Mean
January .	85·9	58·6	72·3
February .	87·1	60·0	73·5
March .	86·2	56·3	71·3
April . .	81·2	53·6	69·9
May . .	74·6	47·4	61·0
June . .	67·6	30·2	45·3
July . .	68·6	31·5	46·7
August .	72·3	44·9	58·2
September	71·1	47·0	59·1
October .	76·0	52·4	64·2
November	84·9	52·9	68·9
December	93·3	58·0	75·7

Rainfall: It is a summer rainfall. The averages for the last ten years have been:

Year	Inches
1938	25
1939	20
1940	26
1941	24
1942	29
1943	26
1944	31
1945	20
1946	18
1947	31

The average rainfall per month over the same period was:

Month	Inches	Days
January .	4·88	12
February .	4·58	13
March .	4·24	11
April . .	1·04	5
May . .	0·00	0
June . .	0·15	2
July . .	0·64	3
August .	0·32	2
September	1·06	7
October .	2·85	15
November	2·00	14
December	3·24	10

Superimposed on the seasonal nature of this rainfall, precipitation is subject to irregular features which lessen its effectiveness. Thunderstorms are characteristic, and a disproportionate percentage of the total annual precipitation occurs in torrential downpours, giving a heavy loss in run-off. Furthermore, the evaporation rate is high. The prevailing winds in the area are from the north-west.

(b) Environs of the Farm

(i) *Towns*

The farm is situated three miles to the north of Buffelsburg, a town of some 20,000 European inhabitants, with a native location of 8,000. The

11

farm lies a few hundred yards west of the main arterial road which con-
nects Buffelsburg with one of the largest South African cities some 150
miles away.

Since the war this town has developed considerably from the industrial
point of view, and large factories have recently commenced production.
These include the following:

   (i) A tannery employing 100 Europeans and 500 Non-Europeans.

  (ii) A footwear factory employing 600 Europeans and 150 Non-
      Europeans.

 (iii) A sweet factory employing 300 Europeans and 80 Non-Europeans.

 (iv) A textile factory and wool-washery employing 250 Europeans
      and 500 Non-Europeans.

  (v) A tinned food factory employing 200 Europeans and 50 Non-
      Europeans.

Key employees in these factories have been imported from other parts
of the Union and overseas; the remainder have been recruited from the
local population.

For the past two years training schemes have been in operation at the
local Technical College to improve the quality of the labour recruited in
this manner.

The industrial development of this town has had a beneficial effect on
the social and civic amenities available to the local inhabitants, viz. a new
City Hall and Municipal Office Building has been erected, which houses
also the Public Library containing some 50,000 books. The old hospital
has been completely renovated and modernized. Up-to-date equipment
has been purchased and a new wing added to the old building, which has
now given 'accommodation to a new dental section, a physiotherapy
department, and office for the Public Health Centre established under the
National Health Services Scheme.

Because of the new industrial demands for light, power and water, the
Electricity Supply Commission has erected a new power station to serve
the area, and the municipality has nearly completed a new reticulation
scheme on the Western River, which will meet the increased demands for
water supply, and allow also for further industrial expansion in the future.

With the town's population increasing rapidly new demands have been
created for sporting facilities and public amusement. As yet no expensive
cinema has been built, and the existing 'bug-house' has proved so un-
attractive beside the splendour of the new civic buildings that the population has preferred to make its own amusement. In consequence many
flourishing societies have sprung up in recent months, e.g. a Repertory
Society, a Film Society, a Debating Society, and several Adult Education
Study Groups, etc., etc., which all enjoy the amenities of the City Hall.
A new Sports Club Building has been completed and the grounds for a
variety of sport are being laid out at present.

Thus, the general atmosphere in the town is one of blossoming pros-
perity. The only factor which seems to stand in the way of unlimited
development is the paucity in the supply of immediate labour, particularly
Non-European.

(ii) *Surrounding district*

The town of Buffelsburg is situated in the heart of an agricultural district. The main types of farming undertaken in the area are: dairy-farming, sheep-farming, maize, fruit and vegetables. The industrial expansion in the town of Buffelsburg has had both a beneficial and an adverse effect on farming in the area, which had shown signs of falling off. In the first place, the farmers are now assured of a ready market for their produce and by-products, which they had previously not enjoyed. On the other hand a supply of reliable Native labour is becoming more and more difficult to obtain. It seems that fate is offering them a golden opportunity with one hand, while at the same time depriving them of the means to take full advantage with the other. The situation has reached a stage where only the intensive mechanization of farming methods will enable the farmers to keep pace with the ever-increasing demands of the factories and local townspeople.

(c) *Finances*

(i) *Initial capital outlay*

Cost of farm	£15,000
Houses for 30 ex-volunteer families	£75,000
Community centre building	£8,000
Community centre amenities	£2,000
Administration building and offices..	£4,000
Physiotherapy and sick bay building	£3,000
Physiotherapy and sick bay equipment	£3,000
Workshops and equipment	£6,000
Farm buildings	£6,000
Farm equipment and materials	£4,000
Water works	£8,000
Sewerage and roads	£4,000
Contingencies	£2,000

N.B. The above figures were only put down as a guide by the Council, and need not be rigidly adhered to by you as manager.

(ii) *Estimated annual expenditure*

Salaries: Permanent European staff	£8,000
30 Native labourers	£1,440
Materials and equipment	£900
Administration and overhead expenses	£1,000
Wages to 30 ex-volunteers	£6,480
Maintenance of buildings	£320

(iii) *Subsidization*

The Foundation, assisted by the Government, is prepared to subsidize the scheme, in perpetuity, to the following extent:

(a) It will pay the salaries of the permanent European staff.

(b) It is prepared to contribute an amount of £14 per man per month in the industrial aspects of the scheme.

(c) In addition it is prepared for the first three years, until full production is reached, to lose an annual amount, not exceeding £5,000, on the agricultural aspects of the scheme.

After this period it is hoped that, by the efficient utilization of the resources available, plus the subsidy granted, the *whole* project will be made self-supporting.

ASSIGNMENT

Having been acquainted with the policy of the National War Memorial Foundation, and supplied with relevant information about its project and the environment in which it is intended to flourish, you will appreciate that there are many problems with which you will be faced, and for which you will have to plan with great care.

These problems can be categorized as follows:

(1) The planning and layout of the whole scheme (situation of buildings, houses, roads, farm lands, etc.).

(2) The planning of the type of buildings and houses to be erected.

(3) The agricultural activities to be undertaken, methods to be used, and facilities to be provided.

(4) The industrial and quasi-industrial activities to be undertaken.

(5) The planning of the finances of the scheme.

(6) The social and cultural activities of the Community Centre.

(7) The educational and training methods to be adopted for the re-training of ex-volunteers.

(8) The method of selecting eligible ex-volunteers for the scheme.

(9) The health and therapy arrangements necessary for the Community Centre, and the rehabilitation of disabled men.

(10) The allocation and appointment of suitable staff to run the scheme, and the provision of office administration.

(11) The organization of maintenance and engineering services.

(12) The publicity and public relations arrangements.

You are required to make a close study of the material with which you have been provided, and to choose *any three* of the above problems on which you would be prepared to pilot your recommendations through a committee.

To-morrow you will be given *one* of these *three*, and asked to act as chairman of your group whom you will have to persuade to accept your recommendations.

You will be allowed twenty-five minutes in the chair.

You must remember that questions will naturally arise in committee which will have a bearing on aspects of the scheme, other than those which you have chosen for special study. You must, therefore, look at the scheme as a whole. If you do not do this you will not be in a position to answer the criticism of others.

Remember also that it is important that you do not sit back while others are conducting the committee's proceedings. You will also be judged on your ability to criticize effectively the recommendations of others (when they are in the chair), and to contribute to the formulation of final decisions.

ANNEXURE G

Your Name...No....................

SOCIOMETRIC QUESTIONNAIRE

This is a test of your ability to judge or size up other people.

We have given you all a number of tests and observed you in many situations, and we have a pretty good idea of the kind of people you are. Now we want to discover what is the correspondence, or lack of correspondence, between the judgements which we have formed of you, and the opinions which you have formed of each other.

We give you this test because we believe that the success of whichever job you will carry out at the Corporation will depend in large measure upon your ability to judge others accurately.

Instructions

Here are a few questions for you to answer about the members of your group. Think about the men carefully before you answer the questions. Then answer each question by putting down the *numbers* of the men whom you choose. You may mention as many men as you wish in answering each question.

Do not hold back any honest opinion.

(1) With whom would you enjoy continuing your acquaintance?

....

(2) Which men expressed the most realistic and convincing opinions in the discussion yesterday?...

(3) If you were given the responsibility for picking men who would have to work together in an administrative office, which members of the group would you exclude because of difficulties in getting along with others *over a period of time*?...

(4) Whom would you recommend as supervisor of a group dealing with problems of planning and organization?...

(5) Whom would you be inclined to avoid socially?...

(6) Which men are the most inconspicuous, i.e. least noticeable?

....

(7) Which men seemed to get along most easily with the other members of the group?...

(8) If you were a member of a committee, whom would you prefer to act as chairman?...

(9) Which men seemed to antagonize other members of the group?

....

(10) With which member/s of the group would you prefer to work as a junior member of their staff?...

(11) Which other member/s of the group would you choose to serve as a junior member of your staff?...

(12) Which men, if any, annoyed you by talking too much, in being too dogmatic in their statements?...

BIBLIOGRAPHY

ANSBACHER, H. L. (1941). German Military Psychology. *Psychological Bulletin*, 38, 370–392.

ARBOUS, A. G. (1951). A Note on the Concept of Test Reliability. *Bulletin of the National Institute for Personnel Research, South African Council for Scientific and Industrial Research*, III, 2, 1–9.

ARBOUS, A. G. (1953). *Tables for Aptitude Testers*. National Institute for Personnel Research, South African Council for Scientific and Industrial Research.

ARBOUS, A. G., & MAREE, J. (1951). The Contribution of Two Group Discussion Techniques to a Validated Test Battery for the Selection of Administrative Personnel. *Occupational Psychology*, XXV, 73–89.

ARBOUS, A. G., & SICHEL, H. S. (1952). On the Economies of a Pre-Screening Technique for Aptitude Test Batteries. *Psychometrika*, 17, 331–346.

BEVERSTOCK, A. G. (1949). Group Methods applied to Youth Leader Selection. *British Journal of Educational Psychology*, XIX, 112–20.

BIESHEUVEL, S. (1945). The Civil Service Selection Board. *Aptitude Test Section (South African Air Force), Memorandum to the South African Public Service Commission of Enquiry*.

BION, W. R. (1946). The Leaderless Group Project. *Bulletin of the Menninger Clinic*, 10, 77–81.

BRIDGER, H., & ISDELL-CARPENTER, R. (1947). Selection of Management Trainees. *Industrial Welfare*, XXIX, 177–81.

BURT, C. (1942). Psychology in War: the Military Work of American and German Psychologists. *Occupational Psychology*, XVI, 95–110.

DAVIES, J. G. W. (1950). What is Occupational Success? *Occupational Psychology*, XXIV, 7–17.

EATON, J. W. (1947). Experiments in Testing for Leadership. *American Journal of Sociology*, LII, 523–35.

FARRAGO, L. et. al. (1941). *German Psychological Warfare*. New York: Committee for National Morale.

FRASER, J. M. (1946). An Experiment with Group Methods in the Selection of Trainees for Senior Management Positions. *Occupational Psychology*, XX, 63–7.

FRASER, J. M. (1947). New-Type Selection Boards in Industry. *Occupational Psychology*, XXI, 170–8.

FRASER, J. M. (1950). New-Type Selection Boards: a Further Communication. *Occupational Psychology*, XXIV, 40–7.

GARFORTH, F. I. de la P. (1945). War Office Selection Boards. *Occupational Psychology*, XIX, 97–108.

GILLMAN, S. W. (1947). Methods of Officer Selection in the Army. *Journal of Mental Science*, XCIII, 101–11.

GOODENOUGH, F. L. (1936). A Critical Note on the Use of the Term 'Reliability' in Mental Measurement. *Journal of Educational Psychology*, 27, 173–8.

HARRIS, H. (1949). *The Group Approach to Leadership Testing*. Routledge and Kegan Paul, London.

HEARD, A. O. (1946). The Growth and Development of War Office Selection Boards. *Paper read to British Psychological Society, Scottish Branch*.

HOOVERS (1948). Selection of Supervisors: an Account of a Procedure Developed by Hoovers Ltd. *Journal of the Institute of Personnel Management*, 30, 3–7.

KELLY, T. L. (1942). The Reliability Coefficient. *Psychometrika*, 7, 75–83.

KUDER, G. F., & RICHARDSON, M. W. (1937). The Theory of the Estimation of Test Reliability. *Psychometrika*, 2, 151–60.

LOEVINGER, J. (1947). A Systematic Approach to the Construction and Evaluation of Tests of Ability. *American Psychological Association Monographs* No. 285, 61, 4.

McCLELLAND, W. (1942). *Selection for Secondary Education*. University of London Press.

McNEMAR, Q. (1949). *Psychological Statistics*. John Wiley & Sons, New York.

MERCER, E. O. (1945). Psychological Methods of Personnel Selection in a Woman's Service. *Occupational Psychology*, XIX, 180–200.

MORRIS, B. S. (1949). Officer Selection in the British Army. 1942–1945. *Occupational Psychology*, XXIII, 219–34.

MORRIS, B. S. (1950). A reply to Colonel Ungerson. *Occupational Psychology*, XXIV, 58–61.

MURRAY, H. A., & MACKINNON, D. W. (1946). Assessment of OSS Personnel. *Journal of Consulting Psychology*, 10, 76–80.

MURRAY, H. A., & STEIN, M. (1943). Note on the Selection of Combat Officers. *Psychosomatic Medicine*, V, 386–91.

OSS ASSESSMENT STAFF (1948). *Assessment of Men: Selection of Personnel for the Office of Strategic Services*. Rinehart & Co., Inc., New York.

PEARSON, K. (1931). *Tables for Statisticians and Biometricians, Parts I and II*. Cambridge University Press.

PONS, A. L. (1951). *A Critical Analysis of the Trial Interview Test*. Unpublished Thesis, Rhodes University College, South Africa.

REEVE, G. (1949). The Validation of Boards, Observers and Selection Procedures. Chapter XX of HARRIS, H. (1949) above.

REEVES, J. W. (1950). What is Occupational Success? *Occupational Psychology*, XXIV, 153–9.

RODGER, T. F. (1948). Personnel Selection. Chapter 16 of HARRIS, N. G., *Modern Trends in Psychological Medicine*. Butterworth & Co., Ltd., London.

ROFF, H. E. (1948). Selecting for Management. *Journal of the Institute of Personnel Management*, 30, 224–31.

ROTTER, J. B., & WILLERMAN, B. (1947). The Incomplete Sentences Test as a Method of Studying Personality. *Journal of Consulting Psychology*, II, 43–8.

SICHEL, H. S. (1948). The Application of Statistical Quality Control to Aptitude Testing. *Bulletin of the National Institute for Personnel Research, South African Council for Scientific and Industrial Research*, I, 1, 22–4.

SICHEL, H. S. (1950a). Note on Reliability of Combination of Sub-Tests, Tests or Criteria. *Bulletin of the National Institute for Personnel Research, South African Council for Scientific and Industrial Research*, II, 2, 57–60.

SICHEL, H. S. (1950b). The First Peace-Time Validation of Army Selection Tests with a Discussion of Some Statistical Problem Encountered in This Project. *Bulletin of the National Institute for Personnel Research, South African Council for Scientific and Industrial Research*, II, 1, 4–35.

SICHEL, H. S. (1952). The Selective Efficiency of a Test Battery. *Psychometrika*, 17, 1–39.

SICHEL, H. S., & MARITZ, J. S. (1950). *Bulletin of the National Institute for Personnel Research, South African Council for Scientific and Industrial Research*, II, 2, 61–7.

SISSON, E. D. (1946). What War Department Psychologists Do. *Army Information Digest*, I, 46–51.

SISSON, E. D. (1948). The Personnel Research Programme of the Adjutant General's Office of the United States Army. *Review of Educational Research, Special Edition*, XVIII, 575–614.

SKELLAM, J. G. (1949). The Distribution of the Moment Statistics of Samples Drawn Without Replacement from a Finite Population. *Journal of the Royal Statistical Society, Series B*, XI, 291–6.

STOTT, M. B. (1950). What is Occupational Success? *Occupational Psychology*, XXIV, 105–12.

SUTHERLAND, J. D., & FITZPATRICK, G. A. (1945). Some Approaches to Group Problems in the British Army. *Group Psychotherapy*, 205–17. (Beacon House Publishing Coy., New York.)

SYMONDS, P. M. (1947). The Sentence Completion Test as a Projective Technique. *Journal of Abnormal and Social Psychology*, 42, 320–9.

TAYLOR, H. C., & RUSSELL, J. T. (1939). The Relationship of Validity Coefficients to the Practical Effectiveness of Tests in Selection: Discussion and Tables. *Journal of Applied Psychology*, 23, 565–78.

THORNDIKE, R. L. (1949). *Personnel Selection: Test and Measurement Techniques*. John Wiley & Sons, New York.

THURSTONE, L. L. (1931). *The Reliability and Validity of Tests*. Ann Arbor, Edwards.

UNGERSON, B (1950). Mr. Morris on Officer Selection. *Occupational Psychology*, XXIV, 54–7.

VERNON, P. E., & PARRY, J. B. (1949). *Personnel Selection in the British Forces*. University of London Press.

VERNON, P. E. (1950). The Validation of Civil Service Selection Board Procedures. *Occupational Psychology*, XXIV, 75–95.

WILSON, N. A. B. (1948). The Work of the Civil Service Selection Board. *Occupational Psychology*, XXII, 204–12.

W.O.S.B. TECHNICAL MEMORANDUM (1942). *Diary of Technical Developments.* No. 1/1, 15 June.

W.O.S.B. R.T.C. TECHNICAL MEMORANDUM (1943). *Follow-Up of W.O.S.B. Cadets at O.C.T.U., Interim Report.* R.T.C./9. June.

W.O.S.B. R.T.C. TECHNICAL MEMORANDUM (1944). *Principles of Officer Selection.* 18 August.

AUTHOR INDEX

SUBJECT INDEX